HAUNTED
Salem

Strange Phenomena
in the Witch City

Rosemary Ellen Guiley

STACKPOLE
BOOKS

0 11557 00756 5

Published by
STACKPOLE BOOKS
5067 Ritter Road
Mechanicsburg, PA 17055
www.stackpolebooks.com

Printed in the United States of America

10 9 8 7 6 5 4 3 2 1

FIRST EDITION

Cover design by Wendy A. Reynolds

Illustrations on pages 56, 68, 90, 106, 112, and 114 by Marc Radle

Library of Congress Cataloging-in-Publication Data

Guiley, Rosemary.
  Haunted Salem : strange phenomena in the witch city / Rosemary Ellen Guiley. — 1st ed.
      p. cm.
  Includes bibliographical references.
  ISBN-13: 978-0-8117-0756-5 (pbk.)
  ISBN-10: 0-8117-0756-3 (pbk.)
  1. Haunted places—Massachusetts—Salem. I. Title.
  BF1472.U6G86 2011
  133.109744'5—dc22
                                        2010049151

Contents

Acknowledgments   v

Introduction   1

HOW SALEM GOT ITS GHOSTS   **5**
  The Origins of Salem   6
  The Witchcraft Panic   10
  The Cursed Aftermath   20
  Blood to Drink: The Curse of Sarah Good   29
  The Curse of Giles Corey   34
  Explaining Ghosts and Hauntings   38
  The Strange Energy of Place   45

HAUNTED PLACES   **53**
  SALEM   **54**
    Lodging   **54**
      Hawthorne Hotel   54
      The Inn on Washington Square   58
      Morning Glory Bed and Breakfast   62
      The Salem Inn   64
      Stephen Daniels House   73
    Eating Establishments   **75**
      The Great Escape   75
      Lyceum Bar & Grill   76
      Rockafellas   77

Places to Visit   **81**
   Cinema Salem and Museum Place Mall   81
   Crow Haven Corner   82
   Gallows Hill   85
   Hex   86
   The House of the Seven Gables   88
   Joshua Ward House   93
   Old Jail Site   93
   Old Witch Gaol Site   95
   The Ropes Mansion   97
   Salem Athenaeum Library   99
   Salem Common   100
   Salem State College Mainstage Theatre   101
   Salem Witch Museum   104
   Salem Witch Trials Memorial   105
   Witch Dungeon Museum   107
   The Witch House   107
   Witch Trials Site   109
Cemeteries   **110**
   Broad Street Cemetery   110
   Howard Street Cemetery   111
   Old Burying Point   113
   St. Mary's Cemetery   116
   St. Peter's Episcopal Church Cemetery   117

DANVERS   **119**
   Danvers State Hospital Site   119
   Danvers Witch Trial Memorial   121
   Rebecca Nurse Homestead   122
   Samuel Parris Home Site   126
   Whipple Hill   129

LYNN   **130**
   Dungeon Rock   130

MARBLEHEAD   **134**
   Old Burial Hill   134

Bibliography   137
About the Author   138

Acknowledgments

I am deeply indebted to four persons who were instrumental in making this book a reality. First and foremost, my thanks to Lori Bruno and Christian Day for their hospitality and generosity, enabling me to make extended stays in Salem for my research. Lori, a Sicilian Witch, offers readings at Hex, one of Christian's haunted shops in the center of town. Christian also owns Omen, and has sponsored me for speaking engagements and book signings there. Christian has long been instrumental in promoting Salem's tourism, and has organized some of the city's Halloween celebrations, including the Festival of the Dead. Both Lori and Christian shared their insights into Salem's haunted side.

Tim McGuire, who owns Salem Night Tour, one of the city's leading ghost walks, generously shared many of his experiences and anecdotes concerning Salem's hauntings, including little-known details. Tim, a longtime resident, knows Salem inside and out.

My friend Fiona Broome, a fine paranormal investigator and author who has researched many places in Salem, shared some of her experiences and findings. Of particular interest is her work on the ley, or energy, lines in Salem, which I consider to be very important in the "why" of some of the hauntings. Her findings and map are featured in the book.

Also crucial to my research were the key people in some of Salem's most haunted places who graciously granted interviews and access: Laurie "Lorelei" Stathopoulos, the owner of Crow Haven Corner; Kevin Marchino, a partner in Rockafellas; George Harrington, owner of the Lyceum Bar & Grill; Diane Pabiche, co-owner, and Yuscenia Sutton, office supervisor, of The Salem Inn bed-and-breakfast; Bob Marcey, innkeeper, and Paul Stream, manager, of The Inn on Washington Square; Bob Shea, owner of the Morning Glory bed-and-breakfast; and Kay Gill, owner of the Stephen Daniels House.

Finally, but not least by any means, I would like to acknowledge the influence of Laurie Cabot, "the Official Witch of Salem," whom I first met in the 1980s while researching my *Encyclopedia of Witches, Witchcraft & Wicca*. Since the early 1970s, Laurie has worked to put Witchcraft and Witches on the map in Salem. She established Crow Haven Corner, now owned by Lorelei; taught classes in Witchcraft; established the Witches Ball at Halloween; and spearheaded many other activities that restored interest in Salem's witchcraft heritage and promoted the renaissance in Witchcraft in general. At a time when few people stood out on the streets, Laurie wore her striking black Witch's robe everywhere—and still does. Laurie gives readings at The Cat, The Crow, and the Crown, her shop on Pickering Wharf.

Introduction

Few cities in America fascinate as much as Salem, Massachusetts. Founded in part as a place of religious refuge, Salem rose from a harsh and austere beginning to world prominence as a sailing port. But the religious oppression that many of the early settlers sought to escape in their homelands became a weapon that they turned upon themselves. The result was the worst episode of witchcraft hysteria in the New World, the Salem Witch Trials of 1692–93. Hundreds of people were accused of black magic crimes, and many were jailed and tortured. Nineteen were hanged, one was crushed to death, and at least four others died while languishing in a filthy prison awaiting their trials.

The witchcraft hysteria has eclipsed most other highlights of Salem's history. When people think of Salem, they automatically think of witches. For years, modern Salem sought to shake that legacy, until it was promoted in the 1970s through the efforts of Wiccans, Witches, and Pagans. Some embrace the witchcraft legacy and others still do not, but the economic fact remains that Salem's witchy history draws more than one million tourists every year. (In keeping with the preferences of modern Witches, I have capitalized the term when referring to modern people who practice Witchcraft as a religion. When referring to earlier witches, who were considered sorcerers, I have used the lowercase.)

Alongside the histories of the witches, the Puritans, and the maritime glory lies an incredibly rich legacy of ghosts and hauntings. Salem and the surrounding areas are packed with ghosts. The land had its own supernatural foundation long before the Puritans arrived. The settlers imported their native folk and religious beliefs and superstitions, and embedded them into the land. Historical events—not just the witchcraft hysteria, but also wars, battles, and the tribulations and triumphs of everyday life—have added to the ghostly lore. All of those factors happen everywhere, but there is something peculiar about Salem: it spectacularly retains the memories and imprints of much of its past, to be experienced as ghosts, hauntings, and paranormal phenomena by those who live and visit there.

Salem has intrigued me for many years, ever since my first visit there in the mid-1980s to research the witch history for my *Encyclopedia of Witches, Witchcraft & Wicca*, and then the ghost lore for my *Encyclopedia of Ghosts and Spirits*. There is a palpable energy of place that sets Salem apart, a brooding feeling that bridges the past to the present. The experience of that has brought me back time and time again. Looking for ghosts involves much more than the thrill of the supernatural—it is one way that people stay connected to, and experience, the events and emotions of the past. In a curious way, ghost hunting keeps the dead alive in our collective memory.

While I was researching this book, I was the guest of both Christian Day, owner of the Hex and Omen shops (both are featured here for their hauntings), and Lori Bruno, a Sicilian Witch who gives readings at Hex. Both of them live in old homes near the center of town. At Lori's, my guest bedroom was on the second floor of the late-eighteenth-century house. Almost every night I was awakened around 3 A.M. by the sound of tapping in the room. It was a sharp sound, as though someone were striking a hard surface with something equally hard. It was not a dull thump like you might hear against a wall.

One morning I asked Lori, "So who's the ghost here?" I knew nothing about the history of the house.

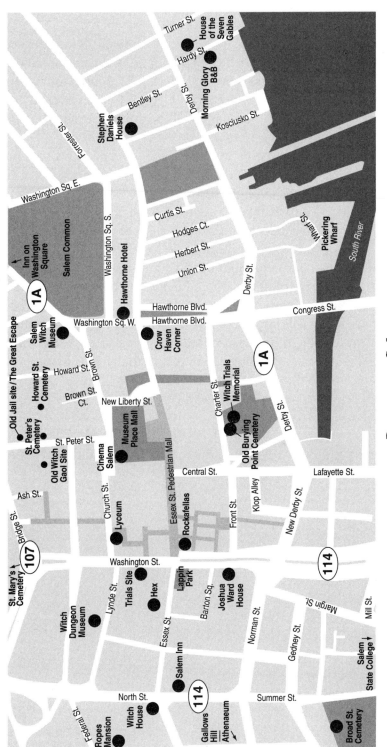

Downtown Salem

Lori laughed. "So you heard him, too," she said. "Almost every-one who stays in that room hears the tapping." She explained that the ghost is the man who built the house, John Ropes, and he taps at night when he likes the guests. I guess he approved of my research! Ropes is also a namesake of the famous Ropes Mansion featured in these pages.

This book will acquaint you with the history of Salem that has helped to create the town's haunted personality, and will guide you to thirty-six places of ghostly note. I have visited every one of them, and have investigated at some of them. There are many more places to be discovered, and perhaps you will find them in the course of your own paranormal explorations.

I also delve into explanations for hauntings, including some theories of energy of place, which I believe to be quite important to the haunting equation.

I have spent a great deal of time in Salem over the years, and it never grows old in its mystery and mystique. I hope this book opens the door to an enduring interest in the city, its history and heritage, and in the ghosts that linger still.

HOW SALEM
Got Its Ghosts

The Origins of
Salem

The seeds of Salem's haunted history were planted with the first footsteps of colonial settlers upon the land. Salem was named after the Hebrew word for peace, *shalom*, but peace was scarce in the formative years that led up to the explosion of the witch hysteria in 1692, the event from which many of Salem's present-day hauntings were born.

The founders of Salem came from Plymouth, Massachusetts, which had been settled mostly by English religious refugees who sought separation from the Church of England. Some of the Plymouth settlers were unhappy with the degree of separation established in the New World. They wanted to distance themselves from what they saw as the corruption and tyranny of the Church, but not necessarily the Church itself.

In 1625, Roger Conant and Reverend John Lyford became dissatisfied enough with the attitude of Plymouth to seek out a new settlement. They established Cape Ann, which did not succeed, and most of the settlers who followed them there went back to England. In 1626, Conant sailed along Cape Cod to the mouth of the Naumkeag River and established another colony. The settlement was originally called "Naumkeag," a local Indian term meaning "eel land," but its name was later changed to Salem.

A small band of people followed Conant, and most of them settled along what became Essex Street—a line through Salem that, as we shall see, was to become very important in the town's history and hauntings.

Dissention among the population broke out immediately. Living conditions were harsh, and there was great fear of the Indians. Lyford decided to move to Virginia, and some departed with him. Conant persuaded the rest to stick it out in Naumkeag.

In 1628, England recognized the Massachusetts Bay Colony as an official body with a governor, John Endicott. Some were unhappy with this, feeling Conant should be governor. Conant was instead named agent of Naumkeag. There were also bitter disputes over whether to raise tobacco. The first settlers were in favor, while some who came later opposed it because they considered it injurious to health.

In 1629, about two hundred new settlers from England arrived in Salem, followed by about seven hundred in 1630. By that time, disease and harsh conditions had taken a serious toll. The newcomers who got off the ships were met by a ragged, unhappy band of people who were in poor health and begged for food. It was not exactly the welcome wagon the immigrants expected. But settle in they did, joined by more immigrants. By 1637, Salem's population had swelled to more than 1,000 people. It spread out over a considerable territory, encompassing present-day Marblehead, Danvers, Peabody, Wenham, Manchester, and parts of Topsfield and Middleton.

Harsh Discipline

The Salem Puritans were a severe, no-nonsense bunch. Behavior that was not tolerated included intemperance, jealousy, slander, nagging, theft, smoking and using snuff in public, cursing, swearing, card playing, lying, fighting, backbiting, idleness, and disrespectful attitudes and language. Devotion to church was to be strictly observed. Public whippings and standing in stocks for small infractions were not uncommon. The whips used were leather with knots tied in the ends to maximize damage to flesh. The victim was left chained to a post to suffer. The stocks, also called the pillory, were slabs of wood with holes cut in them for head and hands. They were set up in public squares so that the punished would be on display for the contempt and ridicule of their neighbors. Another punishment was the ducking stool, a seat at the end of a pole to which the victim was tied and submerged in water several times for long periods.

The Puritans spared no one. Men and women were punished alike. All punishments were carried out in public for the morbid amusement of others.

The Puritans were especially rigid about clothing: everyone was to wear black and dull colors at all times, with no adornments such as lace, ribbons, silks, or bows. Infractions were punished by fines and the stocks. Both men and women were arrested for "dressing too colorfully." Long hair was not tolerated on men.

People had few means of relief from the stress of harsh living. One of the first laws on the books in Salem, in 1628, even banned Christmas! Christmas was to be a day of solemn prayer without festivities, and the governor actually sent spies around to make sure no one was baking, cooking up fancy meals, or otherwise enjoying themselves. Anyone caught doing so risked the stocks, having his ears lopped off, or being excommunicated from the town. Excommunication often meant death, for the victim was run off into the wilderness to face animals, Indians, exposure, and starvation. The excommunicated could not necessarily count on finding sympathy in other towns, where equally severe attitudes prevailed.

There were larger difficulties faced by the settlers as well, such as conflicts with the Crown in England, tensions with the Indians, and struggles against the French. Despite the severity of life, Salem took hold and grew. Money was made in farming and shipping, which in turn created jealous rivalries. The colony attracted immigrants who were more interested in making their fortunes off the New World's riches than in religious philosophies.

Harsh Religion

Regardless of their religious orientation, everyone in Salem was expected to attend church every Sunday. The First Church was established in 1629 at the corner of Essex and Washington Streets. Services were dreary, day-long affairs in which preachers droned on for hours about sin, corruption, and the workings of the Devil, while parishioners were held captive on hard wooden pews. There would be some relief with a break for a midday meal, but then it was back to the pews. Sleepers were prodded with long poles, and persistent offenders were sent to the stocks.

Absolutely no other activities were allowed on Sundays. Records show that a sea captain named Kimbal arrived in Salem on a Sunday, kissed his wife who was at the docks to greet him, and was sent to the stocks for this outrageous display of affection on the Lord's Day.

Anyone foolish enough to complain about the church was whipped, had his ears cut off, was banished into the wilderness, or sent packing back to England. When rival Quakers began to settle in Salem, they were forced to meet in secret. When exposed, they were subjected to tortures and punishment rivaling the worst of Europe's Inquisition, including death by hanging.

Puritan ministers harped on the inborn depravity of humanity, and also kept fears of the Devil alive. The wiles of the Devil were a constant threat, and the arch fiend had seemingly singled out New England as a special target for thwarting souls. The Inquisition, with its persecutions of heretics and witches, was still active in Europe and England at the time when Salem was formed, and supernatural fears were transported to the colony. Influential ministers such as Increase Mather and his son Cotton played on those fears as a way to keep people subdued and in line. The Puritans became even worse oppressors than those they left behind.

In 1664, King Charles of England removed the colony's ban against Episcopalians and gave the right to vote to anyone, regardless of their church, who owned an estate valued at more than forty pounds and who was of good moral character. These measures did little to loosen the Puritan prejudices, which simmered for three decades before boiling over in the witchcraft hysteria of 1692.

The Witchcraft
Panic

By 1692, Salem was well established. Several communities it had once encompassed had split off. Salem itself had split in 1672 into Salem Town and Salem Village (which later became Danvers). Underneath the veneer, however, were tensions, some of them longstanding, that were primed to spark. Despite the Puritans' efforts to keep their community somber and homogenized, class distinctions and attitudes had developed over the years. Salem's people now had a history of rivalries, lawsuits, envy, fortunes, and failures—and very long memories of perceived slights and injustices.

Salem Village now was a separate parish with its own church, but it still remained under the political control of Salem Town. The citizens of Salem Town looked down on Salem Village, which they called "The Farms," because the community was largely made up of farmers—most of whom could barely eke out a living. In addition, Salem Village was torn by two factions struggling for control, creating such rifts that some in the Village rejoined the Town's First Church rather than attend their own. There was widespread fear that the Devil was among them and causing all the trouble.

The ministers of Salem Village had a difficult time mediating the warring factions, as well as trying to make their own ends meet on the paltry salaries allotted them. Some of their wages were paid in farm goods rather than currency. The Village's first two ministers, George Burroughs and Deodat Lawson, both threw in the towel and left town. Burroughs in particular left under a pall of animosity.

The Village's third minister, Samuel Parris, arrived in 1689. Parris was Harvard educated and had attempted to make money in the import-export trade in Barbados. He was not successful, and almost desperate for a regular salary, he decided to become a minister. Various churches turned him down, and finally he applied to Salem Village. He insisted on certain conditions, such as the full title to the parsonage. Even though the Village had not been able to attract a new minister because of its stingy terms, the villagers refused to yield to Parris, and he had to accept their terms with great humiliation. Such a black cloud was not a great way to start his new career, especially in a troubled community.

Parris set up housekeeping in the tiny parsonage with his wife Elizabeth, daughter Elizabeth (known as Betty), niece Abigail Williams, and two slaves from Barbados, Tituba and John Indian (Indian was not their real surname, but an indication of their race). Parris was a humorless man, which fit the grim personalities of the Puritans, and he resolutely tended to his duties. His wife helped him, and the girls were left largely to the care of Tituba. There was little in the sparsely furnished home for entertainment, and the girls depended on Tituba to fill their spare time, especially during the long and cold winters.

A Fascination with Magic

Tituba was an exotic woman full of supernatural stories and folklore from her native country, with which she entertained young Betty and Abigail. One of the things she taught them was how to tell fortunes by the shapes that egg whites took when they floated in a glass of water. It was great fun, but also something that had to be kept secret from prying Puritan eyes—which the girls were unable to do.

In the winter of 1691–92, Betty was nine and Abigail was eleven. They invited their twelve-year-old friend, Ann Putnam Jr., and some other friends and servant girls—Sarah Churchill, Mary Warren, Mercy Lewis, Elizabeth Booth, Elizabeth Hubbard, and Susannah Sheldon—to join their secret activities. All of them were under twenty years of age. Ann's mother and several other married women soon sometimes joined in, attracted by the lure of forbidden magic.

They all took turns fortune-telling for each other, laughing and having a good time. But one day one of the girls saw the egg white take the shape of a coffin, and suddenly the fun was over.

The Mood Darkens

After that, a change came over Betty Parris. She became moody and withdrawn, and in January 1692 she began having hysterical fits in which she would crawl into bed or crawl around on her hands and knees and grunt like an animal. Soon Abigail was affected in the same way. The two complained that invisible sharp objects were being pressed into their flesh. Did their fears get the better of them? It is possible that they had been so saturated with Tituba's stories of ghosts and creepy things that they were finally overwhelmed.

When their bizarre behavior would not stop, Samuel Parris became alarmed and summoned the local physician, Dr. Griggs. He tried medicines, but none gave the girls relief. Griggs came to the only conclusion possible at the time—the girls were under the influence of an "evil hand," that is, a witch who had sent evil spirits to torment them. Word of that diagnosis spread like wildfire through Salem Village.

Parris had an uproar on his hands. He summoned the ministers of the nearby towns to come for a day of prayer and fasting aimed at driving the evil out of the Village. The girls remained afflicted, and the ministers all agreed that a witch was loose among them.

More of the girls became afflicted, including Ann Putnam Jr., Mary Wolcott, and Mercy Lewis. They spoke of seeing witches flying through the winter mist. Putnam's family was prominent and powerful, and vouched for the girls.

Meanwhile, Tituba tried to take matters into her own hands. She followed the advice of a neighbor, Mary Silbey, and baked a rye cake containing urine from Betty and Abigail. She fed the cake to their dog, an action that was supposed to exorcise the evil spirits by sending them into the dog. When Parris learned of this, he flew into a rage and whipped Tituba. He then denounced her and Silbey from his pulpit, accusing them of black magic.

Parris relentlessly questioned the girls to identify the witch who was afflicting them, naming local people until the girls reacted. Betty reacted to Tituba's name. Abigail finally gave the names of two of the Village's least popular women, Sarah Good and Sarah Osborne. The witch hunt was on.

The Siege of Witches

On February 29, Tituba, Good, and Osborne were served warrants and ordered to appear at Ingersoll's Tavern for questioning by magistrates Jonathan Corwin and John Hathorne. A huge crowd of onlookers appeared, forcing the proceedings to be moved to the much larger meetinghouse.

Good and Osborne tried to defend themselves against the charges of witchcraft, but Tituba freely confessed to being a witch and identified the two others as her cohorts. She served up tales of riding to infernal sabbats on broomsticks and poles, and of being badgered by the Devil and his witches to torment the children. The Devil had forced Tituba to sign his book in her own blood, pledging allegiance to him. The revelations sent shock waves through Salem Village.

Tituba's stories were accompanied by fits had by the girls, who were present during the interrogations. Also of special importance were the girls' stories that they were attacked not by the flesh-and-blood persons, but by their specters, or spirit forms, which could also take the shapes of animals. That meant that while the accused persons could be seen going about their daily

The Devil presents poppets to the witches, his loyal servants.

affairs in a seemingly innocent way, their specters were supposedly making evil assaults upon the victims.

Tituba and the two Sarahs were jailed pending trial. Osborne, who was ill, died there on May 10 before she could be tried. Good was tried, convicted, and executed by hanging. Tituba remained in jail until after the hysteria ended.

For eight hellish months, terror reigned in both Salem Village and Salem Town, where many of the actual trials, as well as the imprisonment and executions, took place. One after another, citizens were accused of witchcraft by the hysterical girls, who by this time had accused their entire circle of friends. Some of the accused were unpopular for one reason or another; others were on the winning ends of business deals and lawsuits at someone else's expense. The determination to rout the evil out of the Village was joined by the desire for revenge. Ann Putnam Sr. "cried out" against those on her grudge list. Soon other adults were accusing people, too. Mary Warren had the unique position of being first an accuser, and then a defendant, as she was in turn accused of witchcraft herself. She confessed and was released from jail in June 1692—and went back to work accusing others of witchcraft.

By May 1692 about one hundred accused were packing the jail in Salem Town and people were in a panic. Something had to be done. The newly appointed governor of Massachusetts Bay Colony, Sir William Phips, commissioned a special Court of Oyer and Terminer ("to hear and determine") to oversee the interrogations and trials. The rigid Puritan minister, Increase Mather, was influential in creation of the court and its rules. Although other ministers were against the admission of spectral evidence, Mather, who was convinced that the Devil was afoot in the colony, wrote the rules of the court to allow it. The Court of Oyer and Terminer became the first and only court in America to ever allow spectral evidence in a trial. That meant that an accuser could make up just about any story about being attacked by a spirit or a demon familiar in an animal form—which they did.

Defending one's self against spectral evidence was impossible. Thousands had already died in the Inquisition of Europe as the result of similar evidence. The accused in Salem protested their innocence, but to no avail. Their declarations of innocence were countered by the wild thrashings of the afflicted girls and other victims, who claimed to be attacked even as the accused stood before them in court. It was a show worthy of the greatest drama stage. The victims had little chance of being acquitted.

Residents of other towns beyond Salem were not immune to the charges. The reach of the accusers spread far and wide—even to present-day Maine (then part of Massachusetts), where Salem Village's first minister, Reverend George Burroughs, had gone to live. He was arrested at his own dinner table one evening and taken away to Salem Jail.

Bridget Bishop

Bridget Bishop was not the first Salem resident to be accused of witchcraft, but she was the first to be executed. She was unpopular and an easy target, and her trial, condemnation and execution by hanging were swift.

Bishop, nearly sixty years old, owned a tavern near the Salem–Beverly line. She was lax with some of her customers, who she allowed to stay after-hours drinking cider ale and playing shuffle-board. She drank alcohol herself, and permitted others to drink on Sundays. Bishop had a sharp tongue with her neighbors and was slow to pay her bills. In addition, she dressed in vulgar, flashy ways to show off her well-endowed figure. Bishop had scandalized the locals for years, and now it was payback time.

She was arrested and examined for witch's marks. It was believed that the Devil marked his minions in some way. The tell-tale signs were warts, moles, birthmarks, scars, and such. These were stabbed with pins, and if the victim showed no pain or dis-comfort, it was taken as proof of being infernally marked. Bishop had a growth in her pubic area that passed the test.

There was no shortage of damning testimonies against her. She was accused of driving a woman to suicide, causing a child to sicken and die, making horses balk, causing wagon wheels to fall off, stealing eggs and then transforming into a cat, and appearing in spectral form. A man named William Stacey said she appeared as a specter crouching on his windowsill; the specter then jumped into his room and started hopping about. Another man, Jonathan Lowder, said Bishop tried to choke him, and she took on the forms of a black pig and a monster with the body of a monkey, the feet of a rooster, and the face of a wizened old man. The creature told him it was a messenger from the Devil, and promised him riches in exchange for his allegiance. Lowder tried to strike it with a stick, but it flew off. Lowder then immediately spied Bishop walking through the adjacent apple orchard she owned, implying that the creature was a shape-shifted Bishop.

Most damning of all was the testimony of John Bly, who said Bishop bewitched one of his pigs so badly he had to destroy it. Sometime after this incident, Bishop built a new home and hired Bly to dismantle the cellar of her old home. When he tore down the wall, he said, he found poppets with pins and a hog's bristles stuck in them, hard evidence of her black magic spell casting.

Bishop was found guilty and hanged on June 10, 1692.

Although Bishop's conviction was unsurprising considering her neighbors' animosity towards her, the witch hysteria took an even more dangerous turn with accusations against Rebecca Nurse, a well-respected and pious woman of Salem Village. Nurse was also on Putnam's grudge list. Even the petitions of her neighbors could not save her, and Nurse, age seventy-one, was hanged on July 19. After the fall of such a pillar of society, accusations against others picked up speed. No one—wealthy or poor, pious or outcast—was safe.

The Victim Count

As the summer of 1692 wore on, more than one hundred people were put in jail and nearly two hundred people were accused. More than fifty persons had joined the ranks of the accusers. Confessions saved some from the gallows, but for some of the executed, confessing to something they did not do was unthinkable. Honor and truth were held above death.

The last executions took place on September 22. At that point, nineteen had been hanged; one person, Giles Corey, had been pressed to death, and at least four had died in prison. Families were torn apart, and the lives of countless others ruined. Many had their goods, possessions, and fortunes plundered by the corrupt high sheriff, George Corwin; the son of Justice Jonathan Corwin, George carried out all the tortures and the hangings on Gallows Hill.

Of the nineteen hanged, four were men. Most notable were George Burroughs and George Jacobs Sr. Burroughs was executed on August 19, having been accused of being the ringleader of the witches and a priest of the Devil. Reverend Cotton Mather was especially zealous about seeing Burroughs executed, for he considered him to have unorthodox, and therefore heretical, religious beliefs.

As Burroughs stood with a noose around his neck on Gallows Hill, he made a speech and then recited the Lord's Prayer. It was widely believed that no witch could recite the prayer without stumbling, but Burroughs recited it perfectly. Some in the assembled crowd called out for his release, but the afflicted girls shrieked that the "Black Man" (meaning the Devil) had prompted Burroughs. Few believed that the Devil could recite the Lord's Prayer, however, and a near riot ensued. Mather, on horseback, took control and told the crowd that the Devil could change himself into an angel of light if it served his purpose, and so the execution proceeded.

The hanged were not given proper burials, but were thrown into shallow pits on the hill. Robert Calef wrote in his account of the trials, "When he [Burroughs] was cut down, he was dragged by a halter to a hole, or grave, between the rocks, about two feet deep; his shirt and breeches being pulled off, and an old pair of trousers of one executed put on his lower parts: he was so put in, together with Willard and Carrier, that one of his hands, and his chin, and a foot of one of them, was left uncovered."

Jacobs was accused of being a "wizard" by his own rebellious granddaughter, Margaret Jacobs. Margaret did not escape the witch dragnet herself. She was accused and jailed, but not executed.

Those who were hanged were: Bridget Bishop; Rebecca Nurse; Sarah Good; Wilmott Reed; Mary Esty; Martha Corey; Ann Pudeator; Alice Parker; Margaret Scott; Samuel Wardwell; Mary Parker; John Proctor Sr.; Martha Carrier; John Willard; George Burroughs; George Jacobs Sr.; Sarah Wilds; Susannah Martin; and Elizabeth How.

Four accused who died in jail were Sarah Osborne, Roger Toothacre, Lyndia Dustin, and Ann Foster.

The Hysteria Winds Down

The hysteria reached its zenith when the afflicted girls, emboldened by their influence, began accusing more prominent persons. Governor Phips came home from a trip to Canada late in 1692 to find his own wife, Lady Phips, accused of witchcraft. Incensed, Phips dissolved the Court of Oyer and Terminer on October 29.

To take care of the remaining people in prison, Phips commissioned a Superior Court that included five justices, four of whom had served on Oyer and Terminer. Spectral evidence was banned. Without it, juries had to acquit most of the victims. Eight persons were convicted and sentenced to death, but Phips, who had run out of patience, reprieved all of them. The Superior Court sat for the last time on May 9, 1693.

There was no quick recovery for Salem once the trials were over. Guilt and recriminations were quick to set in—and many residents felt they and the entire community had been cursed, by victims and by God. There were plenty of restless souls, the stuff of ghosts and hauntings.

The Cursed
Aftermath

Cursing is serious business. Throughout history, curses have been held to have special, even magical, power to bring harm, ruin, and death to others. The residents of Salem were so fearful of witchcraft that they killed innocent people to avoid evil. Ironically, Salem suffered anyway, through the curses of the innocent who were executed.

The word "curse" comes from the Anglo-Saxon word *cursein*, which means "to invoke harm or evil upon." The act of cursing is ancient, and probably was used in earlier times as a system of justice. The common person rarely had the means of addressing wrongs in court. Injustices were sometimes rectified with curses, pronouncements that a victim will suffer, often in a particular way. Curses can be leveled against families for generations, and even against entire cities, as was the case in Salem.

The effects of a curse do not need to be immediate, but may take years to manifest themselves. Magical remedies exist to break the power of curses, and the pious also believe that prayer and petitions for forgiveness will help as well.

In ancient times, cursing was a part of daily life. If a person had rivals in business, politics, love, or sports, he was likely to try to diminish or eliminate them by cursing them. Professionals were sometimes consulted. In ancient Egypt, curses were written down on pieces of papyrus, a practice adopted by the Greeks and Romans, who often used thin tablets of lead. The curses invoked the powers of spirits or the dead, who were believed to have great supernatural abilities. The papyri or tablets were buried near a fresh tomb, a battlefield, or a place of execution, where the newly dead, full of anger, could be recruited to carry out the curses.

The Romans were especially good at cursing. They did not consider it immoral, but a tool for getting ahead in life. If you wanted to beat the competition for sports glory, money, power, or love, you laid curses on them. If an unknown person stole your belongings or animals, you cursed them by bringing the wrath of the gods down on them. The Romans didn't fool around. They demanded nothing short of destruction of their enemies in a curse. It is quite possible that their collective skill in cursing was one of the factors that enabled the Roman Empire to be created.

The Evil Eye

One of the most feared curses of all is not verbal, but a certain sinister look from the eyes. The evil eye has been known everywhere since antiquity. It is a baleful look that brings disaster and death. The evil eye can be cast deliberately out of jealousy, anger, or malice, or even inadvertently by people who are born with "killer looks." The lingering gaze, especially from a stranger, is considered by many to be deadly.

The evil eye is usually attributed to humans, but in the Salem witch hysteria, the afflicted girls claimed that two dogs in town affixed them with the evil eye, and some of the victims were said to cast withering, baleful looks as well.

Why do Curses Work?

What makes a curse take hold and last? Certainly, not every ill word or thought has drastic consequences. We still don't have a thorough understanding of the powers of our own consciousness. But there are several factors that likely play a significant role in the success of cursing.

Emotional intensity. Emotions seem to be able to lodge in the very fabric of space and time, where they can have a lasting effect on others and on an environment. Paranormal investigators are familiar with the emotions behind many hauntings. Negative, angry, and unhappy emotions seem to have more staying power than positive emotions. When a person curses, he is usually angry. Perhaps this is why the deathbed curse is so powerful—a dying person, filled with rage, puts every last bit of strength and energy into the curse. The same can be said of innocent persons facing execution, who are filled with rage and hate over their fate.

Receptivity of the victim. The belief of the victim in the power of the curse may help it last. For example, if a dying man curses the family members gathered around his bedside, the fear may lodge successfully enough so that bad things do happen. Family curses can be passed down for generations before they lose power. After the trials were over, people in Salem felt guilty and cursed for their sins of killing the innocent.

The beliefs of others. If a curse becomes well-known, the beliefs of outsiders may contribute to its powers. If visitors know a place is supposed to be cursed, they may feed the curse and keep it active. Interestingly, it often doesn't matter if the events behind a curse are real or embellished folklore. If enough people believe, the curse takes on its own real power.

Geophysical factors. When a place or land is cursed, there may be something literally in the landscape that energizes the emotional energy and keeps the curse alive. There may be some composition of rock or soil, for example, that somehow feeds the power of curses and hauntings.

Curses of the Salem Witches

In the superstitious climate of the American colonies, cursing took a deadlier turn. Any bad luck could be blamed on a witchcraft curse. If a person had an argument with a neighbor and then suffered illness or misfortune, the neighbor might be suspected of cursing or spell casting. Simply harboring unfriendly thoughts about someone—called ill-wishing—was a form of cursing, and therefore witchcraft.

The residents of Salem Town and Salem Village had their share of disputes and disagreements, and inevitably some felt wronged. When the witchcraft hysteria started, it was all too easy to remember harsh words said in the heat of an argument, or some business deal gone bad, and decide that a witch's curse was behind the anger.

But instead of ridding themselves of curses, the accusers brought curses down on their heads—often with disastrous consequences.

WILMOTT REED

When it comes to curses, people have long memories. One of the executed victims was Wilmott "Mammy" Reed (also spelled Redd), who lived in nearby Marblehead and was married to a fisherman named Samuel Reed. Folks in Marblehead regarded Reed—who was believed to have worked as a cleaning woman—as a witch, and kept their distance from her. Her most significant crime as a witch took place five years before the hysteria.

At that time, Reed got into a dispute with Goody Simms of Salem Town. Simms believed she had some laundry stolen by a serving girl living with the Reeds. She went to Wilmott and demanded the laundry back. Reed defended the girl, and the women argued. Simms threatened to go to Judge Hathorne and take out a warrant against the girl. Reed responded by cursing her, that "she would never mingere [urinate] or carcare [defecate] again." The curse reportedly took hold, and Simms soon was ill of a "dry belly-ache" and an inability to relieve herself. The affliction reportedly lasted many months, and Simms was not cured until she went away to the countryside.

On May 31, 1692, Reed was arrested and brought to Salem Village for interrogation. There Reed found herself charged with "Certaine detestable arts called Witchcraft and Sorceries Wickedly

Mallitiously and felloniously hath used practised and exercised At and in the Towne of Salem in the County of Essex," according to the official court records.

Reed had numerous accusers in Salem. Elizabeth Booth said she had been tortured and afflicted by Reed. Booth, Susan Sheldon, and Elizabeth Hubbard fell into fits in her presence. Mary Wolcott and Mary Warren claimed to have been tormented by Reed. Ann Putnam Jr. said she was struck down and choked. Charity Pitman of Marblehead told the court about the curse against Goody Simms.

Reed was among the final eight victims to be hanged, on September 22, 1692. They were herded into an oxcart to be taken to Gallows Hill, and the cart became inexplicably stuck and could not be budged for some time. This only made the townspeople more convinced than ever that all were witches, and the Devil was making a futile attempt to save his servants.

Reed's final curse was leveled against all of Salem: "This town shall burn!"

BRIDGET BISHOP

Bishop, the first to be executed on June 12, 1692, reportedly gave Salem the evil eye during her trial. Cotton Mather wrote that as she was being dragged along Prison Lane to the court to be given her death sentence, Bishop gave an evil stare at the Puritan Meeting House, the first Protestant church in America. Immediately, according to Mather, an invisible demon shot into the church and started wreaking havoc, tearing the place apart. Townspeople, hearing the great noise, rushed in and found a board with a nail affixed to it.

SAMUEL WARDWELL

Samuel Wardwell, of Andover, was a carpenter who had a knack for fortune-telling. Perhaps he had a bit of innate psychic ability. Whenever his neighbors wanted to know something about the future, they asked him. Never mind that fortune-telling supposedly was a gift from the Devil, according to conservative religious beliefs. People always want to know what fate has in store for them, and they are willing to bend the "rules" to do so.

Besides seeing the future, Wardwell also seemed to have an uncanny way with animals, getting them to come to him. And he had an unchecked temper. If he became mad, he uttered the curse, "The Devil take it!"

All of those factors proved to the fearful that he was a witch. Hauled before court, Wardwell broke under the strain and confessed to entering into a pact with the Devil, signing the Devil's book, and being baptized as one of his followers. Although he recanted two weeks later, Wardwell was retried, found guilty again, and was one of the last to be hanged on September 22, 1692. As he prayed in his final moments, the executioner, smoking a pipe, blew smoke in his face, causing him to choke and be unable to finish his prayers.

Curse Aftermath

The end of the trials did not bring an end to Salem's problems. Almost immediately, Salem residents saw they had executed innocent people and felt deeply guilty of sin. As the years went by, the people suffered one misfortune after another. Some of the victims in jail still could not get out, because they had no money to pay for their food and "lodging." The families of the convicted lost their money and property, rendering them homeless and with no means to recover. Those who had been convicted but not executed lost all their civil rights. Houses went to ruin and crops went untended and unharvested. For years, crop failures and epidemics brought misery to the area. Wardwell's frequent curse seemed to come true—the Devil took Salem.

Political changes swept out the old and brought in the new. The Essex County Court declared that the Salem Village committee was derelict in its duties, and ordered a new election for January 15, 1693. An anti-Parris committee was elected, led by the angry Nurse family. Worried about his job, Parris delivered a "Meditation for

Peace" sermon on November 26, 1693, in which he admitted to giving too much weight to spectral evidence. It was not enough to appease the rising guilt and regret in Salem Village. The Village quit paying his salary. Parris's wife, Elizabeth, died on July 14, 1696, after delivering their second child, a son. Broken and realizing he was finished, Parris left his ministry in April 1696 and moved to Stowe, Massachusetts, where he fell into obscurity. Before leaving, Parris sold Tituba to pay for her jail expenses. Nothing is known of the rest of her life, nor of the fate of her husband, John.

Parris married again and had four more children. His son by Elizabeth, Noyes, worked for a short time as a minister and died unmarried and insane at age 49.

Abigail Williams apparently could not let go of her "affliction" and died young. Betty Parris, however, escaped any effects of curses and enjoyed a long life. In 1710 she married Benjamin Barron and moved to Concord, Massachusetts. She died at age seventy-eight on March 21, 1760.

Others on the persecuting end, including Reverends Cotton and Increase Mather, other clergy, the magistrates, and the accusers, suffered illnesses and personal setbacks that went on for years. Increase expressed regret over the trials, but Cotton became more entrenched than ever in his belief that the Devil was tormenting New England.

More and more, residents felt cursed, that they were being punished by God for hanging innocent victims. A new fear took hold of the community, and people tried to lift the curse by making apologies and praying for forgiveness. In January 1696, twelve jurors issued a joint formal apology. They said they had been influenced by the "powers of darkness and the Prince of the air" and were "sadly deluded and mistaken." They humbly begged for forgiveness. Judge John Hale admitted to errors in judgment in convicting several of the victims.

On January 14, 1697, an Official Day of Humiliation of fasting and prayer for forgiveness was held in an increased effort to expiate the collective guilt and sin. Judge Samuel Sewall's daughter had died in 1696, and he believed that her death was punishment for his condemnation of the victims. On January 14, he issued a written apology, read out loud in church, in which he desired to "take the blame and shame of it, asking pardon of men, and especially desiring prayers that God . . . would pardon that sin and all other his sins . . . [and] not visit the sin of him, or of any other, upon himself or any of his, nor upon the land." Sewell spent the rest of his life observing a day of prayer and humiliation every January 14.

Ann Putnam Jr.'s parents, Thomas and Ann Sr., died in 1699 within two weeks of each other. They were forty-seven and thirty-eight, respectively. Death often came at young ages in colonial times, but many of the trial victims were elderly; the Putnams died quite young. Ann Jr., nineteen by then, was left to raise her nine brothers and sisters, who ranged in age from seven months to eighteen years. She never married. In 1706, she publicly apologized for her role in the hysteria and begged for forgiveness, especially for bringing about the death of Rebecca Nurse. Putnam said she had been "deluded by Satan" and desired to "lie in the dust." She died in 1716 at age thirty-seven.

In 1711, reparations were paid to twenty-two families and their survivors.

The curse of Reed took more than two centuries to come true. On June 25, 1914, a great fire swept through Salem, destroying a quarter of the city. The fire started in a leather factory when chemicals exploded. With the region parched by a long drought, buildings went up in flames like kindling. When the fire was over, 1,376 buildings over more than 253 acres were gone. Some 20,000 homes were destroyed, and 10,000 people lost their jobs. Miraculously, only a few people lost their lives.

Still, Salem struggled under a perceived cloud. In 1957, the Commonwealth of Massachusetts pardoned all of the accused and reversed their convictions. In 1992, three hundred years on, the city erected a memorial to the victims. Danvers, the former Salem Village, did the same.

Some residents today still feel that Salem remains stained from its past, a once glorious and mighty shipping port brought down by a slip into the dark side of fear. Others feel that the city has regained its footing.

Mixed feelings continue about recognizing the witch side of Salem, spotlighted by an influx of practicing Wiccans and Pagans who call Salem home, and to the attention given the witchcraft trials in the tourist trade. Not everyone was pleased when in 2005 a bronze statue of Elizabeth Montgomery as the *Bewitched* television witch Samantha Stevens was erected at the intersection of Essex and Washington Streets. Two episodes of the show were filmed in Salem.

The curses told here are probably but a few that were leveled during the heat of the witchcraft trials and executions. Two of the most famous curses, from Sarah Good and Giles Corey, deserve their own stories.

Blood to Drink: The Curse of Sarah Good

onvicted on the testimony of hysterical girls and vengeful neighbors, the condemned witch trials victims had every reason to be full of anger and even hate, prime ingredients for lasting curses. Sarah Good had special reasons: not only had numerous persons come forward to accuse her of witchcraft crimes, but her own husband and four-year-old daughter testified against her. And, she had been grievously wronged in her life. In her final moments, Good leveled a blistering curse that eventually came true.

The injustice against Good was so swift that it must have been staggering to her, even beyond comprehension. Good, along with Sarah Osborne, were the first to be identified as a fellow witches by Tituba Indian. Good was accused of harmful acts against Betty Parris, Abigail Williams, Ann Putnam Jr., and Elizabeth Hubbard. Tituba claimed that Good and Osborne had forced her to appear before Putnam and tried to get her to cut off the girl's head with a knife, a tale corroborated by young Ann. Tituba said she saw Good's name in the Devil's book, and also that she, Good, and Osborne had ridden to witches' meetings on a pole.

Good fit the profile of accused witches, not only in the American colonies, but also of those persecuted in Europe during the

Inquisition. She was an ill-tempered beggar, scorned by neighbors who considered her a pox upon proper society.

Good actually had been born into a family with money. But in 1672, her father committed suicide, and she and her sisters lost their inheritance. Suicide was considered a crime, and the state had the right to seize the assets of a suicide victim. Good went from comfort to being penniless overnight. Back then, there were no social services or agencies to step in and help the poor. Unless an individual took pity on them, the poor were treated as outcasts with little hope of ever improving their lot. If they had debts they could not pay, they were cast into jail until their debts were paid off, which usually required the intervention of someone with money. If the poor did not die in the horrible conditions of prisons, then they most likely died of cold, starvation, or illness.

Desperate to avoid such a fate, Sarah married William Poole, an indentured servant far below her social station. More bad luck followed: William died shortly after the wedding and left Sarah saddled with debt.

Sarah managed to land a second husband, William Good, a timid weaver and laborer. Legally, he was required to pay off her debts. The burden proved to be too great, and William had to forfeit his possessions, including his land and cattle, to his creditors. Homeless, Good and her husband and child lived in barns and ditches and begged for food and money. They were often ignored and refused help. Understandably, Sarah developed a simmering resentment against her neighbors, and often lashed out in anger at them. She was heard to mutter under her breath at them. Sometimes she got back at their stinginess by letting their cattle out of their pens, among other mischief. William developed his own resentments, seeing his wife as the cause of his misfortune.

Thus, Sarah Good—poor, clad in rags, and muttering away—was a prime candidate for witchcraft.

As the hysteria got under way, Good was ordered by judges Hathorne and Corwin to appear for examination on February 29, 1692. She was none too pleased at this latest indignity, and did not hide her displeasure. She was pregnant with her second child at the time, and believed that her condition entitled her to leniency.

She was wrong. Good was put immediately on the defensive by the charges against her. In particular, all her mutterings were interpreted as bewitching and hexing against her neighbors and their livestock.

Good bravely defended herself, firmly stating that she had never harmed anyone. She denied that she was a witch, or owned a familiar spirit in the form of a yellow bird that sucked blood from her right hand. She denied having cat familiars, and denied shape-shifting into the form of a wolf to try to attack Hubbard. She denied ever making a pact with the Devil. "I am falsely accused," she stated.

Early on, she must have felt confident that such ridiculous charges would not hold up under scrutiny. But the judges demanded to know why she did not tell the truth and described to her how they had heard that she tormented the children who started the hysteria. Pressed again and again, Good lamely pointed the finger at Sarah Osborne.

Asked who she served, Good replied that she served "the God that made heaven and earth." This answer satisfied no one. The court clerk, Ezekiell Chevers, noted that "her answers were in a very wicked, spiteful manner reflecting and retorting against the authority with base and abusive words and many lies she was taken in."

William Good seized the opportunity to strike back at his spouse, and perhaps even get rid of her. "I am afraid that she either is a witch or will be one very quickly," he told the judges.

"Why do you say so of her," asked Hathorne. "Have you ever seen anything by her?"

"No, not in this nature," admitted William. "But it is her bad carriage to me, and indeed I may say with tears that she is an enemy to all good." He said his wife had a "strange teat," presumed to be for suckling her demon familiars.

With her own husband calling her "an enemy to all good," nothing but tragedy could follow. The parade of witnesses against Good was relentless. Indictment after indictment was registered. Little Dorcas was bullied into confessing that she had been taught witchcraft by her mother. She said Sarah had three bird familiars:

one black, one yellow, and one unspecified, which Sarah sent to harm the plaintiff children. The pregnant Sarah and daughter Dorcas were sent to jail.

More witnesses against Sarah came forward. Abigail Hobbs said she knew Good was a witch, and had been temporarily struck deaf by her. Mary Warren said Good tried to force her to sign the Devil's book. William Allen said she had appeared to him in his bedroom emitting a strange light. Samuel and Mary Abbey accused her of bewitching their cows and livestock to death, and maliciously threatening them and their children. Thomas and Sarah Gadge accused her of killing their livestock, too.

Susannah Sheldon said the apparition of Good came to her and beat and choked her, and moved objects about. Johanna Childin said the spirit of her dead child came to her and told her that Good had murdered him or her (the sex of the child is not specified in the record), and had given the child to the Devil. Sarah Bibber said the apparition of Good tormented her with choking, beating, pinching, and the sticking of pins into her.

On and on the charges went, accepted without question by the judges. Good remained defiant and refused to confess, but nothing could save her life. She suffered in the deplorable conditions in jail. Her baby was born there, and did not survive.

On July 19, Good was condemned to death, along with Rebecca Nurse, Susannah Martin, Elizabeth How, and Sarah Wilds. Their executions by hanging were carried out by Sheriff George Corwin that same day.

As she was led to Gallows Hill, Good was given one last chance to at least save her soul. Reverend Nicholas Noyes, Salem's assistant minister who officiated at the hangings, urged her to confess to being a witch and repent. Good retorted, "You are a liar! I am no more a witch than you are a wizard, and if you take away my life, God will give you blood to drink!"

Minutes later, her lifeless body was swinging at the end of a rope.

At the time, Noyes probably gave little thought to the angry words of a condemned witch. From his righteous point of view, God's justice was being meted out to the wicked, and evil was being routed out of Salem. When the last hangings took place on September 22, 1692, Noyes regarded the dangling corpses and coldly observed, "What a sad thing it is to see eight firebrands of hell hanging there."

Eventually, Noyes came to regret his role in the hysteria. Perhaps as he got older and the ill fortunes of Salem continued, worry gnawed away at him over the curse of Good. He reached out to help the families of the victims.

It was not enough, for Good's curse struck, in its own time. Twenty-five years after Good cursed Noyes to drink his own blood, he suffered a hemorrhage in his throat, probably an aneurysm, that caused blood to pour into his throat and out of his mouth. Noyes literally choked to death "drinking" his own blood.

The Curse of
Giles Corey

The dying curse of another victim of the witch hysteria has lingered over Salem for centuries. Giles Corey was the only victim to be pressed to death rather than hanged. In fact, Corey remains the first and only person in America ever to be tortured to death in such a manner.

In Salem Village, Corey was a man of means. He ran a prosperous farm and had made good investments with his money. Big and burly, strong as an ox, he also had a mean temper, and he managed to create resentments and grudges. He beat an employee because of his work habits. Another employee unsuccessfully sued Corey for back wages. The case did not go to court but was settled by arbitrators. One of the arbitrators was John Proctor, whose house mysteriously burned shortly after the decision. It is little wonder that some people feared Corey and steered clear of him.

By the time of the hysteria, Corey was eighty years old and had considerably mellowed. He was married to his third wife, Martha, seventy, and the two even attended church together. Martha was considered to be a pious woman, though she had a blemished past—she had borne an illegitimate son. Martha was one of the first victims cried out against by the afflicted girls. When she was jailed, Giles was so distraught that he begged the judges to let him join her there.

He should have remembered the old adage: be careful what you wish for. Soon the girls cried out against him, and he was imprisoned. The girls claimed he had tormented and beaten them, sometimes in apparitional form. Susannah Sheldon said he had two turkeys for familiars, which he allowed to suck at his breast. Ann Putnam Jr. said that she and the other girls "verily believe that Giles Corey is a dreadful wizard for since he has been in prison he or his appearance has come to me a great many times and afflicted me."

Five months after his arrest on April 18, 1692, Corey was brought to the Court of Oyer and Terminer and was asked if he would submit to a trial "by God and his country." Corey refused to answer. His reasons for doing so were never stated, but perhaps he at the least was trying to save his wealth from plundering by the local officials. If he was tried, he would probably be found guilty and would be hanged. If he confessed to being a witch, his property would be seized by the sheriff, George Corwin. (The sheriff had earlier seized the assets of John Proctor, who was executed on August 19.)

So Corey remained silent, to the vexation of the judges. Unless he agreed to trial, they could not try him, and he could not be convicted without a trial. The officials studied the law and decided to torture him in an extreme manner to get either consent or a confession out of him. English law permitted severe punishment by slow crushing under weights, but colonial law forbade "inhumane, barbarous or cruel" treatment. The court decided to turn Corey over to Corwin and look the other way.

Corwin, an anti-witch zealot, was happy to oblige. On September 19, 1692, he had Corey stripped of his clothing and dragged in heavy chains to an open field near the jail (probably where Howard Street Cemetery is today). There Corey was forced to lie down on a wooden plank that had been placed in the bottom of a shallow, grave-like trench. Another plank was put on top of him, and heavy stones and bricks were piled on top of that. Every now

An afflicted witness tells of Giles Corey's alleged wizardry.

and then Corwin would ask Corey if he would submit to a trial, but the old man remained silent. Several times Corwin climbed up on the stone pile himself to add extra pressure.

For two days this horrific torture went on, with Corey struggling harder and harder to breathe, but remaining silent. He was allowed three mouthfuls of bread and three small drinks of water for the duration of the torture.

Once, when Corwin asked if he would submit to a trial, Corey replied: "More weight!"

The pile of stones on him grew higher. Toward the end, Corey's face became bright red, his eyes bulged, and his tongue protruded from his mouth. Corwin took his cane and poked the tongue back in.

Finally the end came. Just before he was fatally crushed, Corey spoke his last words: "Damn you, Sheriff. I curse you and I curse Salem!"

Corey's barbaric death had a sobering effect on the witch hysteria, and was a factor in the decline of the accusations and trials, though more would be executed by hanging before it was all over. Martha Corey was among the last eight who were hanged a few days later, on September 22.

After the trials were over, the townspeople turned on Sheriff Corwin, vilifying and shunning him. In 1696, he had a heart attack and died while still in office. He was in his thirties, a young man even by the standards of the day. The locals said his death was caused by Corey's curse. Corwin was so hated that his family was afraid to bury him in the cemetery, lest his grave be vandalized and his remains desecrated. He was interred in the basement of his home. The site is now occupied by the Joshua Ward House, a privately owned commercial building.

In the years following Corwin's death, people became convinced that every sheriff of Salem was doomed by Corey's curse. In the 1970s, the last man to serve in the office of sheriff (the office no longer exists), Robert Ellis Cahill, investigated the curse and wrote that all sheriffs as far back as he could trace either died in office of heart problems, or retired with "an ailment of the blood." In 1978, Cahill himself was afflicted with a rare blood disorder and suffered a heart attack and a stroke, forcing him to retire.

Corey's ghost is seen in Howard Street Cemetery, and his apparition appears prior to disasters that affect Salem. In June 1914, his bony apparition was seen wringing its hands in the cemetery by multiple witnesses shortly before a fire broke out that leveled a large part of the city. Fittingly, the fire started in the area believed to be the site of the old Gallows Hill, where Martha Corey and eighteen other innocent persons were hanged and buried.

We can certainly see how the turbulent history of Salem and its horrific witchcraft hysteria packed an emotional power that could last for centuries. Do events such as these automatically create ghosts and hauntings? How did Salem get its ghosts?

Explaining Ghosts and Hauntings

A ghost is the presence of the dead. Any life form that has passed on can become a ghost: a person, an animal, a plant, or even an organism. Inanimate objects, such as structures, homes, buildings, machines, and means of transport (ships, trains, planes, cars), can become ghosts. The term "apparition" is sometimes used interchangeably with "ghost"; however, apparition can also apply to something living, such as a doppelgänger, or double.

Ghosts have been with us since ancient times. Most people find ghosts to be frightening or unsettling, for the dead are not supposed to linger in, or return to, our world. Ghosts are not bound by the same physical laws that rule us. They startle us out of sleep or at times when we least expect them. They appear and disappear, yet at times, they appear real and solid. They often seem to be aware of us, but seldom communicate. They have varying behaviors, from drifting about the same places with little apparent awareness of the living, to interacting with us. Most people today believe in the existence of ghosts even if they have had no personal encounters with them.

Ghosts can be experienced in both daytime and nighttime. Ghost hunts are usually conducted at night—it's scarier, for one thing, and perceiving ghosts is often easier in the dark. However, ghosts are around all the time. They are more likely to be noticed when we are in lightly distracted states of mind—and often when we are alone in a haunted place.

How Do Ghosts Behave?

Ghosts seem to have a favorite repertoire of activities. They pull hair, tug on clothing, and tap people, usually on the back. They go past in the form of cold breezes. They make sounds, such as rapping, tapping, thumping, and footsteps. Sometimes they manifest themselves in the sound of heavy furniture dragging across a floor. Ghosts play with lights and appliances, turning them on and off as if the devices were doing so by themselves. They drain the batteries of the cameras and recorders of investigators. They like to flush toilets endlessly, and open and close doors. They whisper into thin air and call out the names of the living who are around. They flit around as white, gray, and dark shadows, and sometimes show up looking like flesh-and-blood people, often dressed in period clothing. Many of these activities have a prankster component to them. Do the dead like to play games and jokes?

Little effort was made to understand the how and why of ghosts until about a century ago. For the most part, ghosts were part of supernatural lore—something that was "out there" to be dealt with from time to time, and to be avoided as much as possible. In the late nineteenth century, the field of psychical research was formed out of an interest in finding proof of the afterlife. The early researchers were scientists, philosophers, classicists, and others. Early research was focused on mediumship, but people's experiences with ghosts and apparitions (of both the living and the dead) were also examined.

The early researchers, such as the founders of the Society for Psychical Research in London and the American Society for Psychical Research in New York City, observed traits about ghosts that have been fairly consistent throughout history. Ghosts are experienced through all five senses, though they most often are perceived through sound, smell, and tactile sensations. A small minority of ghosts are seen. Many people try to capture images on camera. Unexplainable photographs were rare in the past, but our advances in technology, combined with an increase in "ghost hunting," have in recent years yielded many unexplained images. However, we are still far short of proof of ghosts.

POLTERGEISTS

Some ghosts act up and misplace or throw objects, make loud sounds, and create foul smells. "Poltergeist" is a German term for "noisy spirit." Most poltergeists are believed to be non-human, though ghosts of the dead can act in poltergeist-like ways.

Some poltergeist cases have been linked to the living and are thought to be projections of repressed emotions. Some of Salem's hauntings that involve poltergeist activities are of unknown causes or are linked to ghosts. How does a person distinguish between ghost and poltergeist? Sometimes it just isn't possible.

Why are Ghosts Here?

In earlier times, ghosts were thought to be people who came back from the dead or who got stuck in transition and did not make it to the afterlife. If they were the returning dead, they had one of several main purposes: to avenge a wrongful death; to seek closure on unfinished business; to give vital information about their estates not known to the living; to reward the living for good deeds; to remain close to loved ones or a favorite place in life; and to reenact their deaths, or events in their life. If they were stuck, it was because they had died violent or unhappy deaths, had died in sin, or did not yet know they were dead.

These superstitions and folk beliefs about ghosts are widespread. In the case of Salem, these factors might account for the city's ghostly inhabitants. Many hauntings are tied to the witchcraft hysteria, where innocent people died wrongful deaths. Hundreds of people beyond the actual victims were deeply affected, including the accusers, the judges and legal enforcers, preachers, and the silent bystanders who did not speak out against the injustices. Innocent people lost their families, their homes, their properties, and their wealth, and some became outcasts. No wonder their spirits are restless!

Those long-dead people—or at least their memories—may still be here in the form of ghosts. It is difficult, if not impossible, to know for certain, for we still know so little about ghosts. Psychical researchers, followed by parapsychologists and lay investigators, have formulated various other explanations for ghosts beyond the traditional theories regarding returning dead and the stuck.

Many ghosts may be nothing more than imprints, or residues left behind. There is no intelligence or personality animating them. They have varying degrees of activity, and some seem intelligent. Somehow, these residues get pressed into psychic space and become photographs, recordings, and videos of sorts that play when the circumstances are right. Imprints do not react to the living, and often repeat the same action or appearance. Imprints and recordings may be energized into awareness by the consciousness of the living and by the geophysical properties of site—a "place memory."

For example, Frederic W. H. Myers, a founder of the Society for Psychical Research, was among the early investigators who believed ghosts to have no intrinsic intelligence. He defined a ghost as "a manifestation of persistent personal energy, or as an indication that some kind of force is being exercised after death which is in some way connected with a person previously known on earth." Myers did not believe that ghosts were conscious or intelligent entities, but were automatic projections of consciousness that had their centers elsewhere.

More recent researchers disagree, arguing that at least some ghosts possess awareness and react to the living and to the environments they are in. As we shall see later, the energy of place may be a factor in the animation levels of a ghost.

Another explanation holds that part of a person stays behind, perhaps by choice, and interacts intelligently with the living.

Yet another explanation is that ghosts are thoughtforms projected from the living, and perhaps transmitted from witness to witness by telepathy. While it is likely that we participate in hauntings through our interests, it seems unlikely that we create *all* ghosts wholly out of our own minds.

An intriguing theory holds that ghosts may be "time slip" experiences in which the specters are visions of living people from other time periods. They appear as ghosts because they are perceived in an incomplete way. This may account for some experiences in which the witness feels transported to another period in time and sees much more than the ghost—buildings, landscapes, other "ghostly" people, animals, and such. Most people, however, experience a ghost within their own environment in the present, as though the ghost were a visitor or an intruder in the world of the living.

The ghosts of Salem most likely fall into several categories: residual imprints, place memories, psychic recordings, active presences, stuck souls, and time slips.

Who Experiences Ghosts?

Anyone can have a ghost experience, and most people, especially those who go looking for ghosts, are likely to have at least one unexplained encounter in life. People who have a marked and natural psychic ability beyond that of the average person are more likely to have ghost experiences, and more of them. However, it is not necessary to be "psychic," per se, in order to experience a ghost. Belief in ghosts is not a requirement, either. The most hardboiled skeptics and disbelievers can encounter a ghost.

Ghosts are not democratic—that is, when they manifest, not everyone present experiences them. This peculiar characteristic has made it difficult for investigators to establish proof of ghosts. Two people can enter a haunted place, and one person can have profound ghostly experiences while the second person experiences little or nothing at all. Thus, accusations of ghosts being "all in the head" have been leveled by skeptics for many years. However, the variations in perception actually may be influenced by an individual's ability to tune in to subtle phenomena. This ability may in turn vary significantly, due to a host of factors including mood, health, energy, mental distractions, and even environmental conditions.

The bottom line is that we cannot discount personal experiences. Most of what we know about ghosts comes from subjective, eyewitness reports.

What is a Haunting?

A haunting is created by the repeated manifestation of unexplained phenomena, such as apparitions, strange smells, odd noises, temperature fluctuations, and poltergeist activity. A haunting is specific to a place, such as a home or building, or to a general area. Salem, for example, is renowned as a haunted city because so many places within it have paranormal activity. However, not every place in Salem is haunted—at least not at a level noticeable to people.

The word "haunt" comes from the same root as "home." Many people think that deaths are necessary to create a haunting, but this is not so. Death is only one reason why a ghost might inhabit a spot. Emotionally charged events such as battles, accidents, crimes, and suicides can create hauntings too. Pleasant events such as dinners and social activities can also leave behind ghostly imprints, as can places where people were happy. Most hauntings, however, seem to be tied to violent and unhappy events. Perhaps the intensity of negative emotions has more power to last. In addition, some hauntings are aimless, meaning they have no apparent cause. Actually, everything living has the potential to leave a ghostly imprint behind when it dies.

There are no predictable patterns to a haunting. Not everyone experiences the same phenomena. One person may see, hear, or feel a ghost, while others may experience less or even nothing at all. It seems we all have our own built-in "paranormal radar" that has varying degrees of sensitivity. Persons who engage regularly in ghost hunting and paranormal research find that their sensitivity increases over time.

Some hauntings last for very long periods of time, even centuries. Others seem to be short in duration and fade away. There could be a host of reasons why, such as the energy of place, the initial power of the origins of the haunting, and the ability of the living to tune in. We have collective interest in certain places and periods of history, and the energy of this attention and interest may literally supply power to the supernatural phenomena. Hauntings may be one way that we stay connected to our past. We are fascinated by the witch trials of Salem, and so the ghosts of the past are accessible to us. But how many of us are fascinated with Neolithic peoples known as cavemen? We have no idea where to go to experience them, even if we are interested. Their ghosts may be present, but on such a low level that we cannot connect with them.

Actually, I believe that there is not one square inch of this planet that does not hold some level of ghostly imprint from the "blood and the bones" that have gone into the soil. It is fortunate that we do not connect with the imprints left behind of everything that has ever lived on Earth, for we would surely feel pushed right out of our own space.

In addition to events, there is another important factor in why hauntings happen: the energy of place.

The Strange
Energy
of Place

I became aware of the significance of place in haunting activity early on in my paranormal investigating activities. Hauntings are traditionally associated with events, often traumatic, that took place in the past. However, a newly built home can be just as haunted as an old home. No tragic or unusual event needs to have taken place. The key is something peculiar about the land itself.

Have you ever visited a place that seemed to be unusually charged with energy? Sacred sites and mysterious places, such as certain mountains, deserts, rock formations, springs, lakes, wells, valleys, and so on, have radiated a natural attraction to people since ancient times. People feel closer to the gods, so to speak, or to the spirit world, and choose these locations for constructing temples, altars, monuments, and chambers for facilitating the human experience of the spiritual. All sorts of experiences are reported in these places, where just being at that locale seems to open up human consciousness to something beyond this physical world. Sometimes these charged places are left alone but are known to be haunted, such as by spirits, ghosts, fairies, or other mysterious beings and creatures.

These charged places serve as interdimensional doorways or intersections—places where realities collide or blend together. Quantum physics holds that we exist alongside parallel dimensions that are part of our universe. Though right next to us, these realms are usually beyond our five senses, and so we go about our daily affairs oblivious to the teeming worlds just beyond the brush of an elbow or the blink of an eye.

Who lives in these other dimensions? Perhaps there are duplicates or near duplicates of ourselves and our world. They may also be home to everything we consider "paranormal"—ghosts of the dead, alien beings, spirits, gods, angels, fairies, mysterious creatures, and more.

We can get glimpses of, and experiences with, these other realms under the right circumstances. Sometime we just have to be in the right place at the right time. There are a variety of factors that converge to make a haunting, and each of these factors may be weighted differently depending on the situation. The energy of place can be quite significant, merging with the residual imprints of history and events that have taken place in a location.

Over the years of investigating many haunted places, I have noticed certain characteristics that crop up again and again in highly active areas. Some of them deal with terrain, such as places where rivers converge; places adjacent to large bodies of water; pronounced magnetic anomalies due to the presence of iron, magnetite, and quartz; high quantities of limestone and clay; mining tunnels; natural caves and caverns; subterranean springs and water; and swampy and marshy areas. The US Geological Survey's maps of magnetic properties show that Salem and the surrounding areas, including the towns of Danvers, Marblehead, Lynn, and Peabody, sit atop an intense negative magnetic anomaly—that is, the magnetic fields there are significantly lower than the average. It may be that certain magnetic fields act as a battery or enhancer for haunting activity, and help phenomena to stay active for long periods of time, even centuries.

Ley Lines

Another significant characteristic is the presence of ley lines, or earth energy lines. Leys are corridors of natural energy that flow across landscapes, sort of like energy power lines. Leys are believed to influence paranormal activity along them in either positive or negative ways. They are especially powerful where they cross each other, like a crossroads of energies that can either clash or blend well. The earth is crisscrossed with leys, and many have been identified and plotted. The work usually is done by dowsing, which is the sensing of natural energies with rods or pendulums. Leys play a role in decisions made by people throughout history for the placement of sacred altars, temples, and so on. They may even affect the luck and prosperity, for better or worse, of those who live within their fields.

Leys have probably been around since the day the Earth was born, but it was not until 1925 that they were identified and described. Alfred Watkins, an English beer salesman and amateur antiquarian, first mentioned them in his book, *The Old Straight Track*. Watkins said that all holy sites and places of antiquity are connected by alignments of leys: mounds, barrows, tumuli, stones, stone circles, crosses, pagan churches, legendary trees, castles, mottes and baileys, moats, forts, earthworks, and holy wells. Watkins used Ordnance Survey maps to plot them out. Leys, he said, were originally "old straight tracks" that crossed the land-scape of prehistoric Britain, and represented early man's activities.

The ancient men of the leys, called Dodman surveyors, mapped out the tracks for trade routes, astronomical sites, and holy sites by following natural horizon features such as peaks and visual alignments of other sacred sites.

John Michell, a prehistorian who later expanded on Watkins' theory, found that almost every site he visited in England was in perfect alignment with two or more other sites sometimes built at the extreme limit of visibility so that only a tip might be seen above the horizon. Michell further noted that such major holy sites as St. Michael's Mount and Bury St. Edmunds are connected by straight lines travelling over long distances.

Today dowsers detect ley centers, which are often found over magnetic fields or blind springs. Since 1925, England's ley lines have been well identified and plotted on maps. Other parts of the globe also have been plotted for leys, including parts of the United States.

The Judge's Line

A significant ley runs straight through the heart of Salem, along Chestnut and Essex Streets. Essex Street was in the center of old colonial Salem, and it lies in the commercial center of the city today. Chestnut Street is a broad, tree-lined street of elegant homes, many of them built in the nineteenth century by Salem's wealthy and prominent citizens.

Fiona Broome, a paranormal investigator and author who lives in New Hampshire, identified this line. She named it the Judge's Line because of a pattern of homes belonging to judges or persons in the legal profession clustered along it.

"When I study haunted places, I mark maps for every unusual experience, not just ghosts, but also crimes, and just plain weird things that happen. It's not unusual for the plotted points to fall along lines," Broome said.

"I found the Judge's Line by mapping the judicial side of the Salem witch trials. Curiously, that line also indicates where modern-day Salem judges have purchased homes. This line extends directly out from the center of Salem to haunted Gallows Hill Park, the most likely site of the hangings during the Salem witch trials."

Broome has extended lines through Salem and has found another interesting connection to the site of the 1963 murder of Evelyn Corbin. Corbin was the only Salem victim of the infamous Boston Strangler.

"Some speculate that the energy that flows along these ley lines may magnify the emotions or affect the thinking of people when they are on or near the line," Broome said. "The question is, do these lines exist because of the patterns of things that have

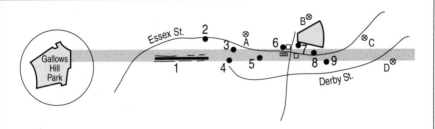

The Judge's Line

1. Chestnut Street (represented by a line). Many past and modern-day judges and elected officials choose this street for their homes.
2. Judge Corwin's home, also known as the "Witch House," from which Corwin condemned many witches during the Salem witch trials.
3. Judge Hathorne's home, also associated with the Salem witch trials. (Nathaniel Hawthorne changed the spelling of his own name to avoid any association with this ancestor.)
4. Sheriff George Corwin's home. George Corwin was the son of the judge (Site no. 2) and benefited by seizing the property of convicted and confessed witches.
5. The home of Samuel Shattuck, whose testimony helped convict Bridget Bishop, one of the first witch trial victims.
6. The home of Massachusetts Bay Colony governor Simon Bradstreet (1603–97).
7. The site of the John Higginson Jr. house. He was the local magistrate. The Hawthorne Hotel was later built on this property. Its guests have reported hauntings, especially on the third and sixth floors.
8. Jacob Manning, a blacksmith whose shop stood here, forged the shackles worn by many witch trial victims.
9. The site of Thomas Beadle's tavern, where witch trial inquests were held.

A. The home of Bridget Bishop, a witch trial victim who may be among the ghosts at the Lyceum Restaurant, now on that site.
B. Ann Pudeator, a witch trial victim whose specter was seen walking along Salem Common, even before her execution.
C. The home of John and Mary English, one of the wealthiest families in colonial Salem. They were accused in the hysteria but escaped to New York.
D. Alice Parker's home, owned by John and Mary English. Parker was accused of witchcraft and put to death.

The slightly triangular area near sites 7 and B represents Salem Common. Gallows Hill Park is indicated on the far left side of the map. The "Judges Line"—indicated in gray—points directly to it.

The small areas near points 6, 7, and 8 represent sites with paranormal activity or were the scenes of violence in the nineteenth or twentieth centuries, or both.

happened—or do the lines influence people to commit certain acts that then result in hauntings?"

We may never know the exact answer to that question. Based on my own research, I believe that both factors are at work. Artificial energy fields such as electricity have been shown to affect us physiologically and psychologically. Natural earth energy affects us the same way. There are places where we feel good and places where we do not; places that uplift us and places that depress us. I have investigated heavily haunted zones and corridors where I have found histories of accidents, illness, violence, domestic strife, financial problems, and bad luck. Perhaps the early settlers of Salem—who already were vulnerable to fear and paranoia about the threat of evil—were subtly impacted by natural forces. The ley energies may not have *caused* the witch hysteria, but may have been one of many influences in the mix.

Essex Street

Essex Street is the heart of central Salem, and it is one of the city's most haunted streets. The pedestrian mall takes up a stretch of the street. Walk into just about any shop and ask about ghosts, and you will probably hear plenty of stories. One of the most frequently cited reasons for the hauntings is the honeycomb of old pirate tunnels beneath the streets. Many of the shops have particularly haunted basements. And, as we noted, Essex Street has an intense history of events related to the witch trials and other important episodes in Salem's history.

The Haunted Places section in this book features several shops in particular: Hex, Omen, and Crow Haven Corner, as well as the Museum Place Mall in general and Cinema Salem.

Also of note are establishments near Crow Haven Corner, which is located at 125 Essex Street. Several shops are housed at 127 Essex Street, among them Remember Salem, Salem Night Tour, and Fool's Mansion. Salem Night Tour is the shop and headquarters for one of Salem's leading ghost walks. Tour owner Tim McGuire has hosted paranormal investigations in his place, often in the basement, where EVP and poltergeist activity are regular occurrences. Clothes have flown off racks and lights go off and on. Disembodied voices are heard, and anyone with a recorder is likely to get plenty of EVP. Mysterious claw marks have been found on the ceiling. McGuire once had his office in the basement but moved out due to the activity. Presently, it is used for storage.

Fool's Mansion is a Gothic clothing store visited by a phantom man in a long black coat and top hat. He is believed to be a former owner who used a back room by the dressing stalls as his sewing room. His ghost is seen there and in the haunted basement, where lights go on and off by themselves. A dark, shadowy form has been seen on the stairs.

Can Science Predict Hauntings?

Scientific research has been done on the geomagnetic and electromagnetic environmental factors at work in haunting. Findings show that energy of place may indeed influence whether or not a place is haunted.

Jason J. Braithwaite, a cognitive psychologist and neuroscientist at the University of Birmingham in England, is among the researchers who have found that unusual and fluctuating natural energy fields are present at many haunted sites and thus may enable a "place memory" of events and personalities to become established. Site energy may especially play a significant role in poltergeist activity.

Scientists do not say that magnetic signatures *cause* phenomena, only that energy and phenomena are associated with phenomena. More study, of course, is needed.

In 2004, Braithwaite and others investigated magnetic signatures at Muncaster Castle in Ravenglass, West Cumbria, a site renowned for its haunting phenomena. In particular, people who sleep in the castle's Tapestry Room report the same phenomena: sounds of children crying and screaming; sounds of adult voices; a sense of a presence and a feeling of being watched; glimpses of fleeting shadows and ghostly figures; sounds of footsteps, raps, and bangs; ringing in the ears; severe headaches; dizziness; feelings of severe foreboding; and the sensation of weight pressing down on the chest and body. Sound familiar? These phenomena are all common to many haunted places.

The study showed that an unusual magnetic field exists in the area of the bed in the Tapestry Room, especially at the bed pillow. If an occupant of the bed moved his head often during sleep, magnetic distortions would occur around the skull.

These are intriguing developments that may help us discover how hauntings really occur. The influences of natural energy do not mean that hauntings are not real; rather, they may open up our sensitivity to the unseen that is around us all the time.

HAUNTED
Places

Here are thirty-six of the most notable and famous haunted places for visiting, staying, and eating in the Salem environs. Most are in Salem proper, and, if you like walking, are accessible by foot from the center of town. Salem's witch history colors most of the haunts, but ghosts aplenty from other periods are around as well.

The witch hysteria actually began in what is now Danvers, a neighboring town a short drive away. I have included several sites there. I also included the famous Dungeon Rock in nearby Lynn, and the elegantly spooky cemetery in Marblehead, which has ties to the witch days.

The majority of these places are open to the public. I have included a few that are not, for one reason or another, but that are important in the haunted history and can certainly be appreciated from the outside.

The listings are grouped by category and are in alphabetical order.

Salem

Lodging

The Hawthorne Hotel

18 Washington Square West

The grand dame of Salem's lodgings is the stately Hawthorne Hotel, built in 1925 specifically to attract tourists to town. Attract them it did, and continues to do so, oozing class and comfort that not only appeal to people, but also to a few ghosts who have taken up seemingly permanent residence.

The idea for the Hawthorne was born in 1921, when the city's movers and shakers saw a clear need for a modern hotel. Plans were drawn up for a six-story, 150-room facility named after Nathaniel Hawthorne. The site chosen was on Washington Square West, next to the beautiful Salem Common, and near three buildings associated with Hawthorne: his birthplace on Union Street (now moved to the House of the Seven Gables); the house on Herbert Street where he grew up and started writing; and the Mall Street home where he wrote his famous novel, *The Scarlet Letter*.

The chosen ground was already occupied, however, by the Salem Marine Society, founded in 1766 as a meeting place for seafaring sailors. In exchange for the tear-down of the existing building, the hotel incorporated new headquarters for the society on top of the hotel, designed as a replica of the cabin of the *Taria Topan*, one of the sailing ships from Salem's East India trade history.

The hotel was constructed in Colonial Revival style in keeping with the mansions along the square. The grand opening in July 1925 spanned three days of ceremonies and the largest parade Salem had seen to date. The city proudly showed off its star attraction, which included a two-story lobby, gracious dining room, and the aforementioned headquarters of the Salem Marine Society.

Over the years, numerous celebrities and important political figures have signed in at the guest registry of the Hawthorne, among them President George W. Bush and his wife Laura; General Colin Powell; newsman Walter Cronkite; and film stars Bette Davis and Vanessa Redgrave. Redgrave lived at the hotel for a month during the filming of *Three Sovereigns for Sarah*, a PBS TV-movie about the witch trials.

The most controversial guests were the cast and crew of *Bewitched*, the 1960s television comedy about a witch, Samantha (Elizabeth Montgomery), who marries a mortal, Darrin Stephens (Dick York). In 1970, a fire at the soundstage where the show was shot created an emergency. The production had to find a place to keep filming while the sets were repaired. The writers developed a series of shows set in Salem, Gloucester, and the surrounding environs. The entire cast and crew set up housekeeping at the Hawthorne, which at that time was called the Hawthorne Motor Hotel. The room assignment records do not survive, but Montgomery and her husband, William Asher, the producer and director of the show, are believed to have stayed in Room 512. The hotel was featured in some of the episodes, and the elevator was used in "Samantha's Bad Day in Salem."

Montgomery and Asher loved the hotel. Souvenirs of their stay—pages of scripts from the Salem episodes and a copy of the special menu served at the Main Brace Restaurant during the production—are still on display in the lobby.

Not everyone in town was thrilled with *Bewitched*, however. Some people felt that the 1692 witch hysteria was a blight upon Salem, and the city should distance itself from any association

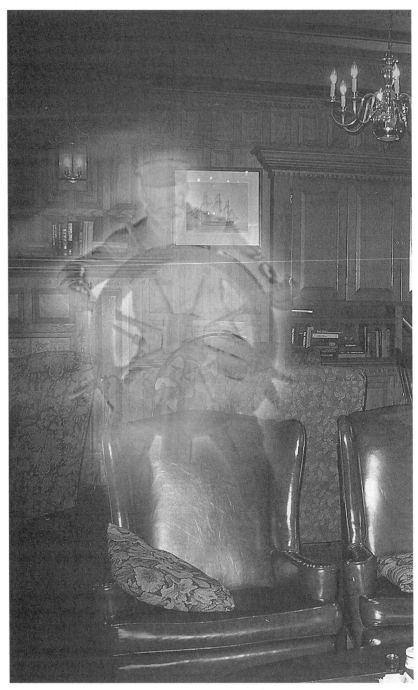

The Hawthorne Hotel

with witches—serious or funny. These critics felt Salem should be identified in the public's mind more with its maritime history than its supernatural history. The critics lost out, however, and a monument commemorating *Bewitched* was placed at the intersection of Essex and Washington Streets at one end of the Salem pedestrian mall.

In the 1990s, the Hawthorne got a facelift. Each of the six floors now has a theme, such as arts, maritime history, and sports. The Tavern on the Green was renamed Parkers, after the toy manufacturer in Salem (now a subsidiary of Hasbro), and decorated with Parker Bros. toys and memorabilia. The Main Brace Lounge became Nathaniel's restaurant. The hotel now has ninety-three guestrooms.

With so much history, it is no surprise that the Hawthorne has ghosts who come along with its charm. In 2007 the popular television show *Ghost Hunters* featured the hotel.

Local lore holds that long before the Salem Marine Society built its headquarters on the site, Salem's first witch to be hung in 1692, Bridget Bishop, had an apple orchard there. Guests smell apples. The exact location of either Bridget's home or her orchard is not known; the apple orchard also was reputedly on the site of another famous haunted hot spot, the Lyceum Restaurant. Nonetheless, phantom apple smells pervade the hotel. Perhaps the smells linger as a residual imprint haunting throughout Salem, a relic of the first execution.

Ghosts of old sea captains and sailors drift around the Salem Marine Society digs and elsewhere in the hotel. Old maps and charts kept under lock and key are sometimes found in disarray in the morning. Perhaps the ghostly seafarers are also responsible for the mysterious actions of the large ship's wheel in Nathaniel's restaurant. The wheel is seen to roll back and forth, as though unseen hands are steering it. In an area known as the "Lower Deck," tables and chairs have been found rearranged.

Room 325, a suite, is active, with bathroom lights and faucets that turn on without human help. The toilet flushes by itself, and the television in the optional bedroom of the suite comes on by itself in the middle of the night. Guests have heard a phantom child crying. Some say they have been touched by ghostly hands.

The elevator made famous by *Bewitched* is believed to be haunted by an invisible presence.

The sixth floor has cold spots and chandeliers that sway soundlessly on their own. Room 612, one of the hotel's suites, features an apparition of a woman who pauses in front of the door while she wanders the hall. Inside the room, the presence of someone unseen is often felt by guests.

One guest and her mother stayed on the sixth floor, and they witnessed their closet door opening by itself, and a shopping bag suddenly crumpling on the bed as though squeezed by a hand. "I've stayed here over a dozen times and this experience still would make me believe this place is haunted," she said.

Some local lore holds that ghosts of the victims of the 1692 witch hysteria executions like to congregate at the hotel. If so, perhaps they are just looking for some creature comfort after their unhappy ends.

The Inn on Washington Square

55 Washington Square North

The Inn on Washington Square is not the only lodging establishment in Salem to be haunted, but it is the only one actually advertised as "A Paranormal Bed 'n Breakfast." Owner Bobby Marcey and manager Paul Stream have had numerous experiences themselves, and they welcome individuals and groups who want to investigate.

The Greek Revival-style inn is a short walk from the haunted Hawthorne Hotel and directly across the street from Salem Common, where the ghost of witchcraft victim Ann Pudeator has been seen. William Hunt, a wealthy merchant in the China trade, acquired the property in 1841. The house was built in 1850. It changed ownership twice before being purchased by John Etheridge, one of Salem's funeral directors, who turned the house into a funeral home.

Bobby and Paul established the property as an inn in 2007. Bobby furnished the inn with many family heirlooms and antiques, giving the place a luxurious Victorian ambience. There are three guestrooms: two upstairs and a large "honeymoon suite" with a Jacuzzi on the main floor. Bobby and Paul have their quarters on the third floor. The honeymoon suite is the most active of the guestrooms.

Prior to their purchase of the property, the two stayed at the house and Paul experienced a first taste of the ghostly activity. Once they were alone in the house and on the third floor, Paul heard footsteps, like those made by hard-soled shoes, coming down the hall. He looked out of his room, but the hallway was empty. Phantom footsteps are still heard from time to time.

Three weeks before settlement, another ghostly encounter happened. Paul and Bobby were sitting at the dining room table going over the contract when a neighbor came in. Paul—who tends to experience more than Bobby—thought the visitor had a man with her. The man was oddly dressed in a black coat, white shirt, and a stovepipe hat. Paul thought perhaps the man was a reenactor. He got a shock when the neighbor took a few steps backwards and went right through the apparition.

After the two moved in, they hung a picture of one of Bobby's aunts on third floor. Paul was admiring it one evening when suddenly the ghost came back. The apparition had both hands clasped onto the lapels of his black coat. The ghost lifted his right hand and pointed at Paul, causing him to bolt down the hallway. Paul searched all the rooms and the basement, but no one else was in the house.

Since that sighting, Paul has seen the figure in other places around the inn, including at the bottom of the staircase. He identified the ghost as John Etheridge, the funeral director, from an old photograph.

Paul has also experienced having his shirt tugged by unseen hands, witnessing a door open and shut by itself, and hearing the sound of childish giggling. Once he saw a tall, thin, shadow figure at the front door. It came in, stopped at the grandfather clock, and then shot up the staircase with lightning speed. Also, a high-pitched voice once spoke out of thin air, "Stop rolling, stop rolling." The meaning of the words was never determined.

Bobby liked to complain in a joking way that nothing paranormal ever happened to him, but in October 2009 he had a dramatic experience that turned the joke into "be careful what you wish for." Paul was witness to it, and to this day Bobby remembers little of it, for he seemed to be in a trance. One night about two weeks before Halloween, Bobby stayed in the honeymoon suite with the dog. Paul was upstairs in his room watching television, and Bobby's father, Arthur, was in another room. Around 3 A.M., Paul's door opened and the light came on. It was Bobby, and he seemed to be sleepwalking. He shuffled in with his head down, shaking from side to side, and his hands clasped as though he were holding his shirt lapels. He was mumbling, "What are all these people doing in my house?"

At first Paul thought Bobby was playing a joke on him, but Bobby was unresponsive. He passed by the bed, left the bedroom, and started down the hallway to the back stairs. Paul became alarmed and went after him. Bobby kept repeating, "What are all these people doing in my house?" His eyes looked like "black pools" trying to focus, said Paul.

Paul slapped Bobby and said in a stern voice, "I don't know who you are, or what you are, but you must leave here *now*." Bobby replied, "I'm leaving, I'm getting out of here." He headed down the back staircase.

Paul roused Arthur, who came downstairs, but Bobby looked blankly at him and said, "I don't know you. I'm leaving, I'm getting out of here."

Paul decided he had better call for help and he dialed 911. Bobby sat down, and then suddenly was back to his normal self, though confused and fatigued. "It was like I was in my body watching a movie," he said of the experience. "I couldn't speak, or do anything with my arms until whatever it was left me. It was like I was possessed. I had a metallic taste in my mouth and I felt nauseated and very tired and drained afterward."

Bobby explained that he had fallen asleep and had a dream in which he watched the wife and child of John Etheridge come up the stairs. They were dressed in period clothing. When they got to the top, Bobby felt a sharp crick in his neck. He remembered nothing of shambling through the hallways, mumbling about people in the house. Had John Etheridge temporarily taken him over? The funeral director was a taller man, and Bobby wondered if the crick in his neck was an effect of a larger presence trying to fit into his body.

In 2008, Bobby and Paul hosted a team of paranormal investigators, the Spirit Seekers of New England. The group, including medium Robyne Marie and EVP specialist Michael Markowicz, documented evidence of the inn's ghostly inhabitants. In addition to Etheridge, the presences include Sarah, a wealthy woman who died in the house; William Hunt, the original owner and builder; two boys named Joey and Daniel; a paperboy who used to deliver newspapers every afternoon; an angry male presence who likes to use profanity; and a male and female couple who like to bicker with each other. The couple, said Paul, once argued about going to a dance; she did not want to go and the man contended that it was the proper thing to do.

In addition, the basement is haunted by a bricklayer named Giacomo, who worked on the house. The back of the basement, which has been added on to the house, has an eerie feel that makes many people uncomfortable, as though they are being watched by unseen eyes.

Numerous EVPs have been captured at the inn—phrases such as "warned you" and "get out" are heard—and investigators have often been touched by ghostly hands. A moving orb of light that acted in an intelligent fashion was witnessed one night in the honeymoon suite by a guest. It floated around the room and then zipped into a dresser mirror and vanished. Guests have heard mysterious tapping noises and whispery voices at night.

Outside in the back, the smell of horse manure sometimes wafts about. There are no stables and no horses, but in the past, when the house was a funeral home, the hearse horses were kept in stables there.

The inn had its grand opening in January 2009. Special packages are offered to paranormal investigators who wish to occupy the entire house.

Morning Glory Bed and Breakfast

22 Hardy Street

This Georgian Federal-style bed-and-breakfast located a stone's throw from the House of the Seven Gables consistently earns top ratings from customers for its comfort and class. There are four bedrooms (one is a suite), and they all come with ghosts. The activity is low-key and friendly.

The Morning Glory originally was a house with a gambrel roof (two slopes on each side) built around 1808. The house was expanded in the 1940s.

Bob Shea, the present owner, acquired the property in 1995 when it was a two-family home. He completely renovated it inside and out in 1996 and converted it into a bed-and-breakfast, a job that took four-and-a-half months. The four guest rooms are each named after a witch trials victim: Elizabeth Howe, Rebecca Nurse, Sarah Good, and Bridget Bishop.

Originally a skeptic about ghosts, Shea has become accustomed to the paranormal activity and to the stories told by the guests. The Morning Glory had been open for about three years when Shea had a dramatic paranormal experience of his own. He was talking to two guests in the dining room about their stay in Salem. Out of the blue the young woman turned to Shea and asked, "Is this house haunted?" No sooner did she get the word "haunted" out of her mouth than a sterling silver teapot sitting on top of an old oak sideboard crashed to the floor. "Coincidence? Possibly," said Shea. "But from that time on I was more open and not as skeptical!"

On one occasion, two women from Montreal, both of whom were clairvoyant, stayed in the Sarah Good suite on the third floor. They sat on the bed and saw the ghosts of young children jumping up and down on the bed. Reportedly, at least three children died in the house in the long-ago past—had they tuned in to them?

A middle-aged husband and wife stayed for three nights in the Bridget Bishop room on the second floor. The room has two windows and a catwalk outside. After the couple returned home, Shea received a note from the wife stating that she had seen a ghost in their room. She woke up one night and was on her side facing the two windows. When she opened her eyes, she saw a young girl of about seventeen with long, wavy blond hair and dressed in period clothing. She mouthed "hello" to the girl, who tipped her head but did not speak. The guest went back to sleep. In the morning, she got up and put on her makeup and brushed her hair. After she put her things down and walked away, she returned to find them relocated.

Another clairvoyant, Rebecca, had an encounter with a ghostly girl who may have been the same figure; her story is on the Morning Glory website:

> We arrived in the late afternoon, and after a few moments of conversation and introductions, Bob showed my husband and me to our room. Not five minutes after Bob left us to settle in, the ghost of a young woman aged approximately 17–20 manifested directly in front of me. She was dressed in a long gown from the late 1800s, early 1900s. It was white, trimmed in royal or dark blue. She had very light brown or dark blonde hair, pulled back off her face but it cascaded over her shoulders. She smiled, and I turned to my husband saying, "That didn't take long." The young woman lingered for a moment, smiling at me, and then slightly nodded to us as if she welcomed us into her home, and then disappeared.

Others who are clairvoyant or psychic often pick up on a female young adult or child, said Shea. "She is a good spirit who is happy with what I've done to the house."

In the Rebecca Nurse room, the phantom of a man has been seen and even photographed. Two women who once booked the room took numerous photographs. One photo shows the room's old mahogany dresser and oval mirror; the profile of a shadowy man dressed in a coat and top hat can be seen in the mirror. "It's clear as day," said Shea. "There was someone else in that room with them."

The ambience and the ghosts keep repeat visitors returning to the Morning Glory every year. Shea collects ghost stories about the bed-and-breakfast from his guests—if you have one, be sure to share it with him.

The Salem Inn

7 Summer Street

A ghost with a fondness for alcohol, footsteps where no person walks, shadows, rattling doors, and disembodied voices whispering in the air are just some of the ghostly activities guests report at the Salem Inn, second in size only to the Hawthorne Hotel among Salem's lodgings. The narrow carpeted hallways and high-ceilinged Victorian rooms are full of mystery, especially in the quiet of the night.

The inn has connections to Salem's witch trials: It was built on land once owned by Jonathan Corwin, one of the judges who presided over the trials, and who lived across the street in what is now known as the Witch House. Did Corwin's land carry a haunted legacy? The parcel does sit along the "Judge's Line" identified by Fiona Broome (see page 49).

If the pathways through the hotel seem like a maze, it is because the twenty-two-room inn began life as three townhouses at 5–7–9 Summer Street. Captain Nathaniel West, a native son of Salem born on January 31, 1756, bought the land in 1811 with money earned through shipping. In 1834, he built three townhouses in elegant Greek Revival style. He also built the historic Phillips House at 34 Chestnut Street for his son, Nathaniel West Jr. The elder West died at number 9 on December 19, 1851.

In the late nineteenth century, number 9 was gutted and turned into ten apartments with Victorian touches. In the mid-twentieth century, nos. 5 and 7 were combined and turned into a men's boardinghouse. In 1983, the properties were purchased by Richard and Diane Pabich, who put the three together and did extensive restoration, retaining the Victorian air. Among the rooms are suites suitable for families; the inn is pet-friendly as well.

The Pabiches own two other bed-and-breakfasts nearby: the Peabody House, built in 1874 as a single-family Dutch Colonial-style home with seven rooms; and the circa 1854 Curwen House, an Italianate Revival with eleven rooms (the Curwen House was placed on the market in 2010). The Salem Inn is also known as the Captain West House.

The Salem Inn exudes comfort, and the ghosts seem to enjoy it as much as the guests. You can spend an evening in the parlor reading the journals kept over the years, in which guests record their experiences, paranormal and non-paranormal alike.

"Our guests have a lot of stories," Yuscenia Sutton, an office supervisor, told me. "The inn often has a strange feeling at night when things settle." Sutton came to the inn in 2004 and got her initiation into the hauntings on her second night of training. She was sent to Room 17 and was greeted by an unusually icy atmosphere. "I opened the door, and it shut behind me on its own," she said. "I opened it and it shut again. There was a weird feeling in the room. I learned later that it was haunted, and one of the *most* haunted rooms in the inn."

For several years, Sutton worked many night shifts, sitting at the reception desk by herself well into the wee hours. "You can see and hear a lot of things when the place gets quiet," she said. "And you learn what's normal for an old building and what isn't."

On many nights, Sutton has heard strange whisperings and whistling above her on the staircase and through the hallways. Early in her employment, she would leave her desk, walk up the stairs, and say, "Hello? Is anyone up here?" There was never anyone about, and the noises would stop as she went up the stairs. Sutton would go back down, and as soon as she was settled back at her desk, the whisperings and whistling would start up again. "It got so repetitive that after a while, I wouldn't even look up the stairs when I heard the noises," she said.

Another common phenomenon was the sound of doors opening and shutting. "They're very heavy, and there is no way they could just open and close on their own," she said.

Small objects get moved around without explanation. "I've put things down and they have disappeared and then shown up in odd places," Sutton said.

The basement where breakfast is served has a spooky feel to it. Sutton, as well as other employees, often does not like to venture down there by herself at night. One of Sutton's night duties was to go down and turn off all the lights. Repeatedly, she would turn off the lights and go back upstairs, and as soon as she was up the lights would all come on by themselves. "I used to call my husband or another office girl to stay on the phone with me when I went down there," Sutton said.

On one occasion, Sutton was alone in the downstairs bathroom. The door to the stall next to hers kept opening and shutting by itself. Sutton assumed it was one of the girls in the office coming down to play a trick on her. When she went upstairs, she said so to her office mate, adding, "Very funny." The young woman looked puzzled. "What are you talking about?" she said. "I've been sitting here the whole time you've been gone!"

Shadowy forms and apparitions have been seen by staff and guests. "When I'm sitting at my computer, I have seen glimpses of a shape walking behind me, reflected in the computer screen," Sutton said. "It appears to be a middle-aged woman. I've turned around and said hello, but no one is there." The identity of the ghostly woman is a mystery, but she has been seen elsewhere in the hotel, including sitting by herself at a table in the basement breakfast room. She likes a spot by the window that looks out onto the courtyard. An apparition reported by guests on upper floors is a man believed to be Captain West.

The Salem Inn has diaries in the Victorian sitting room in the lobby, where guests can enjoy a complimentary glass of sherry and peruse the comments of other guests. The diaries go back several years, and many guests have commented on their ghostly or unexplained experiences. One guest recorded that one evening around 10 P.M., she and her friend were alone in the sitting room reading the diaries when the stopper in the sherry decanter suddenly flew out and fell to the floor with a bang. Evidently, someone or something unseen was trying to get their attention! Another guest said she heard loud music in the sitting room around 10:45 P.M. one night—even though the room has no music player.

In April 2009, paranormal investigators, including Broome, had a chance to hunt for the supernatural at the inn, particularly in the breakfast room and Room 17. In the breakfast room, they documented unusual swings in temperature ranging from five to fifteen degrees below the ambient air temperature. Cyclical cold waves were noted. There were also sensations of heat five degrees or more above the ambient air temperature. Unusual swings in temperature, especially to the cold end, are often experienced in haunted locations, particularly in the spots where apparitions have been seen or activity has been reported.

The researchers obtained names that could be verified in historical records. Some of the names were produced by psychics on the team; others came from a device called the Ovilus, which senses electromagnetic fields in an environment and randomly spits out words from an internally programmed dictionary. Sometimes researchers hear words not in the dictionary, leading to speculation that ghosts or spirits of the dead somehow manipulate the device.

Among the names were Elizabeth, the name of Captain West's wife and one of their daughters; Sarah, another daughter of Captain West; Benjamin, Captain West's brother-in-law; and Dick, the name of the present co-owner of the inn. The researchers heard the name "Catherine" as the female presence in Room 17.

The evidence obtained in paranormal investigations is seldom viewed as conclusive proof of hauntings, but nonetheless, some of it is hard to explain.

Ghostly phenomena happen throughout the hotel. Activity is reported in many of the rooms. The experiences below come from staff and guests, who report events to staff members or record them in the diaries. When the inn is full of guests coming and going, it is sometimes hard to identify paranormal noises apart from natural noises. In the comments below, guests who heard footsteps in the hallways, especially in the middle of the night, investigated and found no person present.

The Salem Inn

ROOM 17

This is the most famous haunted room in the inn. Guests awaken in the middle of the night to see the filmy white apparition of a woman. She is especially appreciative of those who leave out a glass of wine or dark spirits, such as scotch or bourbon. Her identity is not known, but a few years ago the owners found a portrait of a woman behind a heater in the room, and her appearance matches descriptions given by witnesses. She is the same woman seen sitting in the breakfast room, and Sutton thinks she is the one who glides behind her, visible in the computer screen.

Investigators have heard the sound of a gunshot in Room 17, and some of them felt unusual physical heaviness or pain. Guests find their things rearranged and misplaced. Lights go on and off by themselves, the television turns on by itself, and the door to the bathroom closes and locks mysteriously. "My boyfriend's laptop turned on by itself," reported one guest. "The door to the bathroom opened by itself. As I reached for the pack of smokes in my purse, I was amazed and aggravated that they were not there." (She found them later.)

Another guest, who had no idea the inn was haunted, reported: "We arrived late and relaxed in the Jacuzzi. After about fifteen minutes, the lights went out and the TV stopped working. We guessed that the room was haunted and later found out that it was."

Other guests have said they awakened in the night to feel an invisible pressure lying on top of them—not an uncommon phenomenon in a haunted place. Is a ghost trying to get personally close, or does a ghost go to bed too, and lie down on top of whatever or whoever is there?

Things do go bump in the night in Room 17, too. "Twice in the night, the TV remote was knocked off the nightstand," a guest reported. "The second time, it hit the floor so hard the batteries were knocked out."

More than one ghostly visitor seems to like the room. One woman reported in a diary: "My husband was in the shower and I was in bed with my eyes closed. I felt someone sit on the edge of the bed beside me. Thinking it was my husband, I opened my eyes to say something—but he was still in the bathroom. It felt more like a child's weight than an adult weight."

Another guest woke up to a startling sight. "I saw a dark figure in a long coat and a rain hat. I asked him who he was and he said, 'Don't touch me, the dullness rubs off.'" With that, the figure vanished, leaving the witness puzzled by the meaning of the bizarre message.

Sutton discovered on her training night that guests find the room can be unusually cold, even when the heat is turned up. "I was napping in the afternoon, and it was so cold, I turned the radiator up to full," wrote one. "I laid back down. After half an hour the room warmed up, but then it became ice cold again."

Sutton relayed a time when the former innkeeper went to check the Jacuzzi in Room 17. "When she entered the bathroom, the door shut behind her. There is no lock on the door, but it was like it was locked. She could not get out for about fifteen minutes and started to get worried. Then the door just popped open on its own."

ROOM 12

The ghosts or spirits who like this room play with the lights and rattle the doorknob. "The doorknob kept turning like someone was trying to come in," said a guest, "but something was holding the door shut. Then we heard something run into the door, but there was nothing there. Four of us also saw a shadow in the back by the dresser."

"The light in the room came on," said another guest. "We saw shadows pass through the room. We heard a baby crying and a woman sniffling. One of us was touched on the head."

On another occasion, a man heard "a soft female voice" call out his name. When he called back out to his wife, she said she had not spoken a word.

A young guest on her way up the stairs to Room 12 had two odd experiences. "I heard and felt someone going up the staircase, like a rising of skirts before me, but there was no one there. When I got to my room, the door was locked. I knocked and my dad yelled at me to come in, saying the door was not locked. It was. I asked why it was locked, and he said he never locked it."

An entire family got spooked staying in Room 12. "We are hearing noises all over the place—footsteps, a baby crying, a scratching noise. There are bangs coming from the basement. So many things!"

ROOM 13

A guest awakened in the middle of the night to hear the sound of a door creaking open. "I felt pinned down and frozen in bed. There was a pressure near my shoulder, and then something moved across my body as though it rolled from one side of the bed to the other."

Another woman found mysterious things happening to her clothing. "I had planned on wearing a linen blouse one day. Once I put it on, lemony spots kept appearing on it. I'd wash them out and then more would appear. They foamed like soap when water touched them. The next day, there were no spots. But when I got home, there was one on the collar, and it smelled lemony."

ROOM 15

The same "clothing ghost" also affected a female guest in Room 15. "I put on a red blouse and white spots appeared on it," she wrote. "My husband said they looked like soap spots. I decided to wear it anyway. Later I was reading the diaries and saw that someone else had the same problem!"

Apparently the ghost has a problem with women trying to look their best. Another guest was in the bathroom applying makeup when suddenly the makeup case flew out of her hands and hit the wall by the tub. Brown eye-makeup powder spilled out on the wall and fell into the tub.

ROOM 16

Room 16 is the center of frequent activity, judging from reports. "There was a big bang on our door and it opened by itself," said a guest. "I closed it and it reopened by itself two minutes later. Creepy!"

Another reported, "We saw spirit figures in the room. The curtain in the bedroom kept opening after I closed it. If you run the water in the bathroom sink, it shuts off by itself."

"The door handle turned by itself and rattled," a guest said. "We heard knocking in the bathroom and footsteps in the hall."

But perhaps the most remarkable—and poignant—report was made by a man, who said, "The ghost of my dead wife visited me, kissed me three times, and told me, 'Never forget.' And then she faded away."

ROOM 40

Room 40 is host to disembodied voices and a figure who does not want to answer questions. "I woke up about dawn and saw a figure standing on the balcony," said a guest. "I sat up quickly and said, 'Who are you?' The figure was suddenly gone."

A man saw a dark shadow stretch across the ceiling. Was it the same as the figure on the balcony? No one knows.

Another guest experienced "stomping and a muffled voice in the hall outside, and a knocking on the door," as well as "a creaking in the kitchen and a male voice asking, 'What are you doing?'"

Guests also experience haunting phenomena in the Peabody House and Curwen House, though not nearly to the extent as in the Captain West House. Both the Peabody and Curwen Houses are much smaller. Guests in those buildings are served breakfast in the Captain West House. Here are a few comments noted in the diaries:

PEABODY HOUSE

The Peabody House has a bed shaker who seems quite polite. "When we went to bed and closed our eyes, the bed gently rocked," wrote one guest. "This happened three times. Then it felt like someone sat very lightly at the foot of the bed. When we asked it to stop, it did."

Another guest said, "At night my mom got touched on the neck, the TV turned on by itself, and my boyfriend's bed started shaking. Nothing to be scared about. It was really cool."

CURWEN HOUSE

A woman wrote, "My niece and I were taking a nap at about 4 P.M. when we heard what sounded like heavy furniture being moved around on a hardwood floor. We heard knocking sounds on the walls for about five minutes. Later that night we awoke to hear a man's voice and others talking. It was 1:30 A.M."

The sound of heavy furniture moving is a common and quite peculiar haunting phenomenon. The sounds are literally like large chests, armoires, and other furnishings are being dragged or pushed from one end of a room to another. I heard it quite dramatically myself when I stayed in a haunted bed-and-breakfast in Gettysburg, Pennsylvania, and another time in a haunted manor house in Washington State. If you go to investigate, you find a room with nothing out of place, and sometimes not even containing any large pieces of furniture. Do ghosts push invisible furniture about? Or is it a supernatural noise that imitates furniture moving? Perhaps the ghosts are rearranging things in their own dimension, and the sounds just filter into ours.

Stephen Daniels House

1 Daniels Street

This bed-and-breakfast near the House of the Seven Gables and Pickering Wharf is like a trip back in time, and it has attracted quite a few celebrities who have stayed or dined here. It also has some ghostly residents as well.

The three-story, wood-frame Stephen Daniels House is named after the affluent sea captain who built it in 1667. It was enlarged and remodeled in 1756 by Daniels's great-grandson. The house stayed in Daniels family ownership until 1931. The new owners let it sit vacant until 1945, when it was acquired by the Haller family of Oregon. The Hallers restored it and turned it into a bed-and-breakfast with a restaurant. In 1962, Thomas and Kay Gill of Chicago purchased it and continued running it as a bed-and-breakfast. The Gills operated the restaurant for twenty-two years, serving dinner with waitresses dressed in colonial garb. The restaurant is no longer in operation. Thomas Gill has passed on, and Kay continues as the proprietor, serving continental breakfast to the guests.

The furnishings in the house are authentic eighteenth- and nineteenth-century antiques, many of them added by the Gills. The house has four bedrooms upstairs; nine fireplaces, including one in the largest bedroom; and fifty-three windows.

Playwright Arthur Miller and actresses Eve Arden and Elaine Stritch stayed at the Stephen Daniels house, and William Shatner once dined here when he was in town. The Peabody sisters of Salem stayed here. Holly van Praagh, a medium and the former wife of medium James van Praagh, also stayed at the house with her sister.

The ghost of Stephen Daniels is believed to linger on his former premises. In the large bedroom upstairs that features a canopy bed, some guests have seen a phantom man in a shiny black coat and hat. His presence is also felt downstairs in one of the back rooms. One guest who stayed in the big bedroom woke up in the middle of the night, sensing an invisible presence by the bed. Prior to retiring for the night, she had pulled down the blinds on all the windows, but when she awakened again in the morning, the blinds were neatly rolled up. Another guest reported that open windows mysteriously shut by themselves during the night.

A guest saw an apparition of a man in the dining room who looked like one of the portraits hanging on a wall. Yet another guest saw the ghost of a woman fall down the staircase. Perhaps a more careful ghost accounts for the occasional sounds of footsteps going up and down the stairs throughout the night.

The best-known ghost is not a person, but a tabby cat seen by many visitors. The spectral cat zips in and out of the rooms and jumps up on beds, even cuddling up to guests. No one knows the history behind the cat. Gill, who has her own cat, has not seen the ghost herself.

Eating Establishments

The Great Escape

50 St. Peter Place

Once upon a time, inmates at the Old Salem Jail snuck forbidden alcohol to their tiny cells. Now anyone can have a drink there—legally—at The Great Escape, a trendy restaurant that opened in September 2010 in a renovated portion of the original facility. The liquid spirits also come with other spirits—the disembodied kind.

Most of the Old Salem Jail was turned into residential quarters during its recent renovation. The Great Escape owner, Cleber Santos, and general manager, Shane Andruskiewicz, both of Peabody, are the pair behind the new complex's restaurant. The men searched for months for the ideal place to open the restaurant they envisioned, and they found it in the renovated jail.

The Great Escape occupies the area that once housed the sheriff's office. In keeping with the historically correct theme found throughout the residential units, the restaurant features original cell bars, brick walls, high ceilings, and other fixtures from the old prison. Even the granite floor, laid two hundred years ago, is original.

The menu, featuring American food with an Italian influence, features dishes with clever jail-related names, such as Scarface and Mafiosa.

The old jail facility had quite a reputation for being haunted by numerous ghosts and spirits. Staff at The Great Escape claim that some seem to have lingered in the new restaurant. Lights go on and off by themselves. Objects break without explanation. The alarm system has gone off by itself. People feel sensations of being watched, and of cold breezes passing by. Some of the phenomena happen late at night when staff are cleaning up after the restaurant has closed. Sometimes things happen during business hours.

When you go, tune in to the atmosphere and the details of the environment while you enjoy your meal. You might have some invisible company at your table!

Lyceum Bar & Grill

43 Church Street

The ghost of Bridget Bishop is the most famous specter said to haunt this elegant dining establishment. The building is allegedly atop the ground where Bishop once lived and maintained an apple orchard. Other ghostly phenomena have been experienced by patrons as well.

The Lyceum owes its name and some of its heritage to the American Lyceum Movement, which began in the early 1820s. A lyceum is a public hall for lectures, concerts, and programs, intended for the education of the public. Lyceums were popular in England, and an American named Josiah Holbrook thought that such halls would greatly benefit the people of American towns as well, especially the working-class masses.

The Salem lyceum was created in 1830 as the first of its kind in New England. The lyceum became so popular that a permanent home for it had to be created. The land where Bishop once lived was deeded. When the theater was completed, it seated seven hundred persons and was home to two weekly lecture series. The height and footprint of the building are the same today.

For several decades, some of the greatest intellectual stars of the nineteenth century lectured here, among them Oliver Wendell Holmes, Horace Mann, Henry David Thoreau, Daniel Webster, and John Quincy Adams. Alexander Graham Bell gave a public demonstration of the newly developed telephone at the lyceum. The audience was astonished to hear the voice of Bell's assistant, Thomas Watson, speaking through the device from eighteen miles away in Boston. It was the first long-distance phone call.

The lectures gave way to more vaudeville-type entertainment and attendance began to wane in the 1880s. In 1894, the wooden building caught fire and burned down. It was rebuilt on its original foundation as a two-story brick structure and converted into offices. In 1935, the Colonial Café opened in the space that is now the bar.

In 1973, the building was turned into a restaurant, the Lyceum Restaurant and Pub, which was operated for sixteen years by Joan Boudreau. It was purchased in 1989 by George Harrington, who turned it into the Lyceum Bar & Grill. The restaurant and bar are on the first floor. The second floor is used for private parties and events, and also for lectures, in keeping with the original purpose of the place.

Much of the haunting activity takes place on the second and third floors. A ghostly woman believed to be Bishop is seen. On one occasion, two young men were hired to work on the sprinkler system between midnight and 6 A.M. When they were done with the job, they asked if the place had "unusual events." They said that around 2:30 A.M., some empty boxes were thrown down the stairs from the third-floor coatroom and attic by an unseen presence.

Employees have sensed a presence on the third floor, and shadowy figures have been seen in the mirror in the second-floor event room. One cold February night, the smell of apple blossoms wafted through the place. Supplies have sometimes gone temporarily missing, such as a quantity of martini glasses that were later found in an unusual spot.

About sixteen years ago, Lorelei, the owner of Crow Haven Corner, conducted a spirit circle for a private Halloween party and gathering in the Lyceum's second-floor room. A photographer attended and captured some images that appear to be dark spectral figures in attendance alongside the living.

Rockafellas

231 Essex Street

Rockafellas opened as a restaurant in 2003 and inherited a haunted legacy from the famous building it occupies at the corner of Essex and Washington Streets. Regulars and tourists love to relax in the rich, dark wood ambience, or, in warm weather, at the sidewalk cafe. Occasionally they may be joined by an invisible guest. Two that are seen the most are a black-suited minister and a woman in a blue dress dated to the early twentieth century.

The building that houses Rockafellas is the gigantic Daniel Low Building, a cornerstone of Salem commercial history. It was built in 1826 and owned by Salem's First Church. The church used the second floor for worship and rented out the ground floor to businesses in order to defray the maintenance costs. Various enterprises made their homes there, including a crockery, glass, and china shop owned by William Bowditch; a dry goods store owned by Edwin Ide; and a ladies' furnishing store owned by John P. Peabody. The National Exchange Bank took up occupancy in the 1860s, adding a lower-level vault and double-depth windows, still a part of the building today.

Daniel Low opened his jewelry business in a corner room in 1867, an enterprise that was so successful that he soon took over the entire first floor. One of Low's products was a silver souvenir witch spoon of Salem. Its popularity led to him launching the first mail-order catalog business, helping Low's jewelry business become the largest in the world.

Low was a hard-driving man, and he died in the building of an angina attack in 1911. The business was run by his son, Seth, until his death in 1939. Seth's widow, Florence, took over until the 1950s, when she sold the business to William Follett. When Follett died in the 1990s, his children had no interest in the business. Rockafellas, owned by Terence Marchino, Kevin Marchino, and David McKillop, then took over the entire first floor. The church is now long gone, and the second floor is vacant.

Low had built a tunnel between the building and the building adjacent to it that served as his warehouse. The tunnel enabled him to easily move his goods around. Central Salem is riddled with old tunnels, some of them used to hide runaway slaves as part of the nineteenth-century Underground Railroad. Stories are told that runaway slaves who died were buried in the dirt tunnel. When Follett bought the business, he had the tunnel filled with concrete.

Much of the haunting activity at Rockafellas takes place on the tunnel level, where the restaurant staff has its offices and storage areas, but activity also goes on upstairs in the dining and bar areas.

According to lore, a depressed minister back in the church days committed suicide on the property. Another story says that a young woman died in the building, perhaps during the Low manufacturing days. Whether or not the stories are true, and whether or not they are associated with the ghosts who are seen are not known.

Staff and customers have glimpsed the dark-suited, somber figure of the minister. One customer who claimed to be a medium told Kevin that the ghost was trying to communicate with her, but she could not understand him.

The minister is sometimes grumpy, however. One witness who tried to capture him in a photo had his camera jam inexplicably. On another occasion, the ghost was seen downstairs and said, "Git, I don't want to talk to you right now."

Equally striking is the Blue Lady, believed to be one of the women employed by Daniel Low. When Rockafellas had its grand opening, one of the bartenders took a nighttime photograph. It was posted on the restaurant's website and used as a screen saver on the computers downstairs. The ghostly image of the Blue Lady mysteriously appeared on the photo—after it had been posted on the computers and website. Dave McKillop, one of the partners, noticed the image one day on the screensaver. The semitransparent Blue Lady is standing in front of the building, as though she were posing for the original photo.

The Blue Lady became a mascot of sorts for the restaurant. T-shirts proclaiming, "Congratulations—You've Just Seen the Lady in the Blue Dress" were given out to customers who reported weird happenings. The Blue Lady has also been seen in the hallways downstairs, especially by other women.

There seem to be other unidentified spirits roaming about the building, too. Occasionally staff and customers hear random, piercing female screams, both day and night. Kim, one of the bartenders, went downstairs to the vault where the beer is stored. When she closed the door to return upstairs, a loud banging and female screaming emanated from the vault. Kim shot upstairs, looking like she had seen the proverbial ghost. Kevin has heard screaming come from the restrooms upstairs.

Other curious things go on downstairs, especially when staff members are alone. One morning Kevin was by himself downstairs. He took a call for a reservation, and went straight upstairs to enter it into the books. When he returned downstairs, he found that an old, heavy, iron-bar vault door had been shut. The door was so rusted that it could not be budged. Somehow it had shut on its own—without making a sound.

On another occasion, Kevin and the chef were downstairs discussing menus. One of the old chandeliers, a large fixture, was resting on the floor. All of a sudden, the chandelier started shaking violently, as though huge hands had gotten ahold of it. Subways rumble in tunnels beneath the restaurant, but the vibrations could not account for the chandelier shaking and rolling about.

Another mysterious event happened in the bar. Two regulars, a husband and wife, came in and sat at the bar for drinks and dinner. The wife ordered her favorite cocktail, a Cosmopolitan. She took one sip, set the glass down, and started eating her meal. Suddenly the martini glass shattered. Nothing was left but the stem.

Bar glasses do break and shatter, explained Kevin, especially if they go from the heat of a dishwasher straight to ice and cold. However, that was not the case with this glass.

Glass antics entertained another customer and one of the bartenders. A glass from the middle of a stack suddenly went up into the air and bounced down on the counter without breaking.

The ghostly activity at Rockafellas usually occurs when least expected. Though it may spook, it is never threatening or unfriendly. "It's a colorful, fun building," Kevin said.

Places to Visit

Cinema Salem and Museum Place Mall

83 Washington Street

Popcorn and movies go hand in hand, but how about a ghost with your movie? See a film at the Cinema Salem and you might get more than action on the screen. Cinema Salem has a ghostly female who likes to watch the flicks, and she has a favorite seat.

Located in the Museum Place Mall in the heart of town, Cinema Salem is a small complex with three theaters. The ghostly woman likes to frequent theater No. 3, which has 164 seats. She always sits in the back row in the right corner, as you enter the theater and face the stage. She wears nineteenth-century clothing. Perhaps she is mesmerized by modern film entertainment, as she does not seem to discriminate between different types of films—she likes them all.

The ghost is usually seen when the theater is quiet, and especially after hours when the staff is cleaning and locking up for the night. Staff members also say they often feel watched at night, as though someone is standing near them. Perhaps the mystery ghost goes wandering after the patrons have all gone home.

Theater No. 2, which holds 236 seats, is also reputed to be haunted by unseen presences that occasionally make themselves known.

The mall itself has strange phenomena, mostly in the end occupied by the theater, where there are also some shops, restaurants, and the public restrooms. The mall was built in the 1970s; part of the property where much of the activity occurs was once occupied by an arcade. Employees of the businesses in the mall have noticed odd occurrences over the years. Lillee Allee, a psychic who reads at the Omen shop, reports that for years the women's restroom there has had such phenomena as toilets that flush by themselves, and some sort of energy or presence that likes to create disorder. Toilet paper has been seen to unroll itself.

The Omen shop, at 184 Essex Street, sits at a newer end of the mall, with one door that opens into the mall interior and another that opens on the street pedestrian mall. Omen, owned by Christian Day, the proprietor of the nearby Hex shop, opened in 2010 as a psychic reading center, classroom facility, and retail shop. The middle of the shop once had an old exterior wall there, and employees say they can sometimes hear phantom footsteps, thought to be the residual ghostly imprints of pedestrians on the street.

One interesting historical note is that the land now occupied by the mall—and in particular the corner where the cinema and restrooms are located—was mentioned in the witch hysteria trial records. Witnesses reported seeing a spectral pig haunting the spot. The pig has not been reported in recent times.

Crow Haven Corner

125 Essex Street

Crow Haven Corner is one of the best-known witch shops in Salem. It was founded in the 1970s by Laurie Cabot, "the Official Witch of Salem," who was instrumental in establishing the Witch/Wiccan/Pagan presence in the city. Located in a heavily haunted area of town, the shop is currently owned by Laurie Stathopoulos, known as Lorelei to her fans and friends. Lorelei is a natural Witch, spiritual clairvoyant, and love counselor who met Cabot and became one of her students.

Lorelei's own psychic and clairvoyant ability was apparent during her childhood in Revere, Massachusetts. She learned how to read tea leaves from her grandmother, and she was reading Tarot cards by age ten. Her mother was an astrologer and taught her about horoscopes. Lorelei came to Salem in the 1970s to train as a professional kickboxer. Cabot's daughters trained at the same academy, and Lorelei struck up a friendship with them and their

Crow Haven Corner

mother. In addition to studying Cabot's Witchcraft courses, Lorelei helped out at the shop. She had an odd feeling that one day she would own it herself, and she joked that it was "her" building.

In 1998, the premonition came true, and Lorelei purchased Crow Haven Corner. (Cabot now has another shop, The Cat, The Crow and The Crown, located on Pickering Wharf.) Crow Haven Corner features witchcraft and magic items and books, as well as supplies for spell casting. Many of the regular customers come to get psychic readings from Lorelei or one of her readers in a private back room decorated in an Egyptian motif.

The building, which includes the living quarters of Lorelei and her son upstairs, has a long haunted history. Of particular note is the ghost of a playful little girl, Annabelle, who likes Crow Haven Corner and also visits Tim McGuire's Salem Night Tour shop a couple doors down the street. According to Lorelei, Annabelle lived in the 1800s, and she liked to dance.

Disembodied voices are sometimes heard at the shop level. Lorelei has heard a female voice that sounds like her deceased mother at the bottom of the stairs. Upstairs, Lorelei says, the house is full of spirits. "The house is happy," Lorelei said of the energy at Crow Haven Corner. "They like what I've done to fix it up." Many of the visitors and customers sense the unseen presences while on premises.

Lorelei conducted a now-famous séance circle at the haunted Lyceum Bar & Grill about fifteen years ago for a private Halloween party on the second floor, one of the most active areas in the restaurant. Lorelei invoked the spirits of her own mother and of Hecate, the Greek goddess of the underworld and magic. Annabelle also visited, as did other spirits.

In attendance was a photographer who took photos of the event. Several of them show what appear to be the ghost of a girl with long, wavy, dark hair, and a dark, shadowy shape sitting at one of the tables—someone perhaps joining in the fun while remaining invisible to most of the guests. The photos are on display at various places around town, including Crow Haven Corner, of course, and Salem Night Tour.

Gallows Hill

Hanson and South Streets

The executions of the condemned witches in 1692 took place at a site called Gallows Hill. The victims were taken by oxcart from the Old Witch Gaol to the hill. There they were hanged from locust trees and thrown directly into a shallow ditch, for it was against the law to give condemned criminals a Christian burial in a churchyard or consecrated cemetery.

No records survive pinpointing the exact location of Gallows Hill. Various sites have been identified as candidates, but the best bet is Gallows Hill Park, a children's park outside downtown Salem at the intersection of Hanson and South Streets. The land was acquired by the city in 1912 and named after the legend of the execution site.

It is doubtful that any bodies are still buried in the ground here. Few remains linked to the victims have ever been found. Bone fragments have been recovered but not tested or identified. Nor has there been any archaeological excavation.

According to lore, the bodies were disinterred by a wealthy man, Philip English, shortly after the witchcraft hysteria ended. English took them to an unknown location—possibly the cellar of an unidentified church in Marblehead, according to one legend. English's wife, Mary, was accused of witchcraft; she died of illness while in prison awaiting trial. English was outraged at the hysteria. A 1770s account reported a mass excavation of bodies that could have been those of the condemned, but the account also mentions a piece of coffin. The condemned were buried without coffins.

Some historical reports claim family members returned at night to dig up their loved ones and take them home for burial in unmarked graves on the families' properties. Rebecca Nurse's body was relocated by her family, and her remains are somewhere on the property of the historic Rebecca Nurse Homestead in Danvers.

There is no memorial at Gallows Hill Park, perhaps because historians are not certain it is the correct location. For decades, tourists have asked to see the place where the witches were hanged—tourists including the Beatle John Lennon, who came to Salem in his black limousine and drove around town looking for the spot.

On October 8, 1992, approximately two hundred persons from sixteen different evangelical churches gathered at Gallows Hill to hold a "Holy Happening" to exorcize what they believed to be "demonic spirits" at the site that were the lingering results of the wrongful executions. The *Salem Evening News* reported:

> Before the formal program of singing and prayer began, a group of close to 100 gathered into a small, tight circle on top of Gallows Hill, raised their arms skyward and chanted, "The curse over Salem with witchcraft is broken."
>
> They then circled the town water tower on top of the hill, which is decorated with the drawing of a witch, and performed a "laying on of hands" on the tower as a sign of spiritual healing.

Whether or not the park is *the* site, residents who live around it report haunting phenomena in their homes, with strange knocking and thumping sounds. The park area itself has a long history of reported mysterious activity, including apparitions and phantom voices, especially at night. Wiccans like to hold ceremonies at the park on Samhain, or Halloween.

Hex

246 Essex Street

The Hex shop is one of the most paranormally active sites in Salem, but not because of residual hauntings by ghosts. The shop has a magnificent, magical, and genuine altar to the dead, where visitors can pay their respects to family, friends, celebrities, and victims of tragedies and crimes. On any given day, spirits both famous and unknown are likely to drop in, called by the prayers and invocations left at the altar.

The altar to the dead was created by the shop owner, Christian Day, one of Salem's leading Witches, in keeping with ancient customs for honoring the dead. When Day opened his shop in 2008, no community or commercial place in town offered a working altar open to the public. Day, who has always believed in the importance of keeping a link to the dead, felt an altar would give Hex a rootsy, earthy edge.

The altar went in place and quickly became a destination point for residents and visitors alike. The shop was fondly dubbed "Spook Central" for serving as a way station uniting the living and the dead. Spirits are drawn in when people pay respects at the altar.

The altar holds images and statues of deities, magical objects, magical signs and symbols, candles, and images of the dead left by the living. No one religion or spiritual tradition is held above another; the altar is universal, and blends spiritual and magical traditions from both the Old and New Worlds. The celebrity piece on the altar is a genuine human skull, nicknamed "Robert" by Day. Robert is actually a partial skull—the lower jaw is missing—but "he" is nonetheless a powerful magical and necromantic tool for connecting with the dead. "Robert transforms the place into a beacon," Day said. "He acts as a bridge to the spirit world."

Visitors can honor the dead simply by writing a name on a small piece of parchment provided and leaving it on the altar. They are welcome to say and leave prayers as well—whatever they think will remember or help the dead. And for those who desire, the Hex staff will assist in magical spell casting.

"We can call on the dead to help us in all our activities," said Day. "We still have a soul connection with them, even though they have passed to the other side. The dead can be like guardian spirits for us." The more the altar is used, the more magical and spiritual power it develops.

At the end of October (the Witch's new year is Samhain, celebrated on October 31), Day conducts a ritual in which the names left on the altar are read aloud and then burned, which sends spiritual energy into the cosmos. After the altar's first year of operation, four hundred names were read and burned in the ceremony. During the second year of operation, the popularity of the altar zoomed and about three thousand names were left on it. There was not enough time to read all the names in the year-end ceremony, but they were prayed over and honored, and all were ritually burned.

Visitors are often moved by the deaths of people they do not know personally. "It was amazing how many people came to pay respects for Michael Jackson," Day said about the celebrity's untimely death in 2009. "Despite all the controversy around him, many people still felt a strong soul connection to him."

More spirit presences swirl around the shop from the readings given by there by Lori Bruno, a Sicilian Witch and medium who has her table next to the altar. The dead often have messages for Bruno's clients, and can make their presences known in dramatic fashion. Bruno monitors the altar and also adds her own magical energy to it.

What can visitors expect? Pay respects at the altar and you may feel presences, get a tap on the shoulder, or even "hear" your name called out. Spirits may even look over your shoulder as you browse around the shop's intriguing array of books, candles, and magical objects and jewelry.

The House of the Seven Gables

54 Turner Street

One of Salem's most popular tourist attractions is the House of the Seven Gables, made famous by author Nathaniel Hawthorne (1804–64). Located on the harbor, the house itself is a ghostly reminder of shipping fortunes made and then lost, a bust blamed on the curse of the witch trials of 1692.

Victim Sarah Good's curse against Reverend Nicholas Noyes— "and if you take away my life, God will give you blood to drink!"— also blighted the Hawthorne family, the descendants of Judge

John Hathorne. At the time he was called to serve in the trials, Hathorne was part of a wealthy family involved in shipping and politics. His father, Major William Hathorne, was a founding Puritan pilgrim of Massachusetts. John Hathorne thoroughly believed in the threat of witchcraft and considered it a great evil. Though he went through the motions of asking skeptical questions of the accusers, he was quite swayed by their testimonies.

Unlike Noyes, Hathorne never expressed any regret for his role in the trials and executions. But in the back of his mind, he surely must have worried about the curse leveled by Sarah Good, and by the hatred shown him by survivors. One of his most embittered enemies was Philip English, whose wife Mary was accused. Mary's health was so affected by her ordeal that she fell ill and died. Philip was shunned by the community and lost his property and wealth. He never forgave Hathorne and the other magistrates and officials, and so in effect cursed them with undying hatred.

The Salem witch trials seemed to tip the fortunes of the Hathorne family. They lost money, power, prestige, and social status. Hathorne's family and descendants blamed him for bringing a curse upon the family, inherited by succeeding generations.

The shadow of the curse still hung over the family more than a century later when Nathaniel Hawthorne was born in 1804 in Salem. Ironically, the family tree by then included a marriage between the English and Hathorne families. Did that magnify the curse?

Nathaniel was born in a house on Union Street in Salem. As a child he had a vivid imagination. His father died at sea when he was just four years old, forcing his mother to move her children to her parents' home on Herbert Street. Nathaniel was often entertained at the home of his cousin, Susannah Ingersoll, who lived in the house that Nathaniel would immortalize.

The house, also known as the Turner-Ingersoll Mansion, was built in 1668 by Captain John Turner. It was originally much smaller, with two rooms and two-and-a-half stories. As the Turner shipping wealth increased, the house was expanded. Turner also added a secret stairwell that Nathaniel would make famous, too.

The House of the Seven Gables

The house remained in the Turner family for three generations. John Turner III lost the family money, and the house was sold to the Ingersoll family. They remodeled the Georgian style, removing gables and adding Victorian elements. When young Nathaniel started spending time at the house, it had only three gables, but Susannah showed him where the other gables had once been located.

Susannah also educated the young Nathaniel about their families' tarnished history. She was appalled that the Turner house had been built with profits from the slave trade. Nathaniel was fascinated by his ancestor's role in the witch trials, and by the legend of Good's curse. He felt it had affected his family during the ensuing years. By the time he entered college and was pursuing his ambition to be an author, he was so suffering from family guilt that his sister persuaded him to add a "w" to his surname. The "w" had been dropped generations before Judge John, but Nathaniel's sister felt that returning it would separate the author from his cursed ancestor. Nathaniel also publicly apologized on behalf of Judge Hathorne and asked for the curse to be lifted.

The psychological effect of the curse is evident in Nathaniel's introduction to his first novel, *The Scarlet Letter* (1850):

He [Judge Hathorne] made himself so conspicuous in the martyrdom of the witches, that their blood may fairly be said to have left a stain upon him . . . I know not whether these ancestors of mine bethought themselves to repent, and ask pardon of heaven for their cruelties . . . At all events, I, the present writer, as their representative, hereby take shame upon myself for their sakes, and pray that any curse incurred by them . . . may be now and henceforth removed.

Even that was not enough to lift the stain. Nathaniel then used the curse in the plot of his second novel, *The House of the Seven Gables* (1851). He used his own family history and the Turner-Ingersoll Mansion as story inspirations.

In the novel, the fictional Pyncheon family suffers from inherited sin related to witchcraft. Judge Pyncheon covets a neighbor's land and uses the charge of witchcraft to get him executed so that he can acquire it. The neighbor, Thomas Maule, curses him on the gallows at Gallows Hill: "Pyncheon, God will give you blood to drink and quench your greed for eternity."

Pyncheon gets the land and builds on it a grand house of seven gables. His gloating is short-lived, for at his housewarming party, Pyncheon chokes to death on his own blood. The family fortunes slide. The curse ends when the land is rightfully restored to Maule's family.

Nathaniel never actually lived at the House of the Seven Gables. In fact, he was living in Lenox, Massachusetts, when he wrote the novel of the same name, drawing on his memories.

Susan Ingersoll lived in the house until age seventy-two. In 1908, the house was purchased by Caroline O. Emmerton, who had it restored and altered. The missing gables were restored, and embellishments were added that conformed to Nathaniel's fiction. The birth house of Nathaniel eventually was moved onto the property and became part of the museum. In 2007, the seventeen-room, 8,000-square-foot house was designated a National Historic Landmark.

Staff at the House of the Seven Gables say the house has no haunting phenomena, but some visitors report otherwise. Spectral figures appear in the windows. Susannah's ghost has been glimpsed in the hallways, and her pale face is seen looking out one of the upstairs windows. Visitors have also seen the apparition of a little boy, believed to be Nathaniel's son, Julian; some people think it may be Nathaniel himself as a youngster. The little boy ghost is heard running around in the attic and playing with toys. Other phenomena are reported in the visitors' restrooms, where faucets turn on and off by themselves and toilets flush on their own.

Joshua Ward House

148 Washington Street

The Joshua Ward House is now a commercial property and is not open to public tours, but it bears mentioning for its haunted history tied to the witchcraft hysteria. The Federal-style house was built long after the trials, in 1784, for wealthy sea merchant Joshua Ward. It was restored in 1978–79. You can walk by it and spend a moment appreciating the history that took place there more than three centuries ago.

The house sits on land once occupied by the home of High Sheriff George Corwin, the man who carried out the arrests, tortures, and executions of the accused victims. Corwin was buried for a while in the basement of his home. Though his remains were removed to the Broad Street Cemetery, Corwin's ghost is said to haunt the Ward property, along with other ghosts.

Phenomena reported there include the ghostly cries of a child, sounds of singing in the attic area, the apparition of a woman, mysterious hot spots, candles that are removed from their holders and melted into twisted S shapes, objects that are moved about, and alarms that go off for no apparent reason.

Old Jail Site

50 St. Peter's Street

The Old Jail in Salem must be distinguished from the "Old Witch Gaol." They are not the same facility. The Old Jail was built down the street from the Old Witch Gaol in 1813 to replace the older facility. At the time, it rightfully was the "new jail," but as it aged and was itself abandoned, it became the "Old Jail."

The Old Jail, located at 50 St. Peter's Street, has been remodeled and converted into luxury apartments. But have the ghosts gone away? The Old Jail had a rich haunting history that makes it worthy of note. The facility stands next to the haunted Howard Street Cemetery. When you visit the cemetery, take a look at the new housing. The ghosts who lodged at the jail may be enjoying a new level of comfort.

The brick jail featured a main jailhouse with more than one hundred cells, a separate jailor's residence, and a wooden barn. When the jail first opened, condemned prisoners were executed by hanging—in the dining room of all places, which had a trapdoor in the floor. The jail operated until 1991, making it the oldest operating prison in the country at the time.

After the facility was abandoned, the hauntings became more noticeable. People saw lights on in the building, even though the electricity had been shut off. Sometimes ghostly faces appeared in the windows, and phantom figures were seen in the courtyard. Ghosts were seen to move through the exterior wall of the old barn. The sounds of talking and screaming emanated from within. Some of the ghosts were said to be those of Civil War soldiers who had been imprisoned there.

One story concerned the apparition of a man holding a candle, reportedly seen in a third-floor window where no floor existed. Tim McGuire, the owner of Salem Night Tour, reports that he liked to tell the story to his groups as a bit of legend. One night, as he and a group of tourists stood outside the old jail, he recounted the story—and the apparition and light actually appeared in the window!

Years went by as the jail sat empty, while city officials debated options for using the property. Besides apartments, there were proposals for a Monopoly Museum; a veterans' facility; a bookstore; a jail museum; a multicultural center; and a restaurant. The city decided the site would be best suited for apartments—a restaurant named The Great Escape was added later (see page 75)—and plans proceeded for the renovation of the building. The ribbon-cutting ceremony took place on May 27, 2010, and tenants began moving in, paying up to $2,700 a month in rent. The twenty-two units feature hardwood floors, brick and granite walls, and large windows with views of the Howard Street Cemetery and the North River. The grounds are nicely landscaped.

Despite the macabre history of the site and a view of a haunted cemetery, there was no shortage of eager tenants. Seventeen units were leased at the time of the grand opening. City and state officials were impressed; State Representative John Keenan, who had once worked at the Old Jail as a prison guard, called it a "glorious moment for the city of Salem."

The renovation of a haunted facility usually affects the paranormal activity. Sometimes the activity increases, as though the ghosts are disturbed. Other times the activity diminishes or even ceases; it is thought that residual imprints get "erased." Time will tell if the ghosts have moved in with the new residents.

Old Witch Gaol Site

10 Federal Street

The jail that housed the accused witches during the witch hysteria of 1692–93 no longer exists, but you can visit a spot where the jail is believed to have once stood, near the intersection of St. Peter's Street—once called "Prison Lane"—and Federal Street. A plaque on the brick building at 10 Federal Street marks the spot, not far from the "Old Jail" that replaced the dungeon in 1813.

The colonial dungeon was cold, foul, and rat-infested. It was built in 1684, the third dungeon built in Salem since 1663. It was constructed of hand-hewn oak timbers and siding, and it measured only 70 feet by 280 feet. It is hard to imagine large numbers of persons held in such a small space, but the comforts of the jailed were not of social concern in those days. There were no bars or locks, for the Puritans accepted their punishment. Anyone foolish enough to escape risked being killed by Indians or wild animals.

The prisoners were charged fees for their food, drink, and "lodging." They were fed salted foods and drink mixed with herring-pickle; as a result, they were in a constant, dreadful thirst. Any items of comfort, such as a blanket or clean clothing, had to be supplied by friends or family.

Despite the grim conditions, the jail was a social gathering place. The jailkeeper sold grog to visitors who came in the evenings to play chess and other games. For a bond of one pound, a prisoner could be released during the day to visit family and friends. The prisoner was required to return at night.

During the witch hysteria, the jail was packed with the accused. Jailers routinely stripped the women of their clothing to examine them and prick them in search of witch's marks. The accused were tortured. The physical and emotional stress overwhelmed many. Elizabeth Cary was locked in eight-pound leg irons and placed in a room with no bed. Distraught, Cary went into convulsions, and her husband, Captain Nathaniel Cary, bribed the jailer with his life's savings in order to get his wife freed.

Elizabeth Cary was not the only accused witch to suffer convulsions; many of the other victims suffered hysterical fits from the conditions and their treatment at the hands of the jailers. Others expired. Two victims, Sarah Osborne and Ann Foster, died in jail. There was no relief in death, for Foster's son was assessed a fee of two pounds, sixteen shillings for permission to remove his mother's body for burial.

There were more indignities to be endured by the innocent accused. They and their families were charged for everything. The salaries and expenses of the sheriff and his staff, the magistrates, the hangman, and all persons concerned with the court were paid by the accused, who were each assessed one pound, ten shillings. In addition, the prisoners were billed seven shillings and sixpence for their fetters, chains, and cuffs, and an extra fee for being searched for witch's marks. The hangman's substantial fee was charged to the victims' estates or families. Those who had money fared the best. Captain John Alden, jailed on witchcraft charges, escaped by bribing the jailkeeper with five pounds. He fled to New York until 1693, when the hysteria ended.

After the accused were condemned, they were taken from the jail by oxcart out to Gallows Hill. Their corpses, swaying from the limbs of the locust trees, could be seen from the center of town.

When the hysteria ended, there were still people in the Gaol. Some of them had no family or means to pay the fees they had accumulated during their incarcerations, and so they were forced to remain. Several languished and died in prison, innocent and technically "free." Other victims' families lost their fortunes after being forced to sell their lands and possessions to pay the jail fees.

In 1764, the jail was expanded with the addition of second and third stories. It was discontinued as a jail in 1813 when a new jail was built closer to the North River. The old Gaol passed into private ownership and was used as a residence. In 1863, it was purchased by Abner Cheney Goodell, state historian; it was later acquired by his son, Abner Cheney Goodell Jr.

The old Gaol deteriorated and was given little historical attention until 1934, when Abner's wife found in an old sealed closet a jailer's bill for the keep of paupers, some of whom were victims in the Salem trials. In response to public inquiries about the dungeon, the Goodells opened the jail to the public in 1935. The building was demolished in 1956. Conditions in the old Gaol are re-created in the Witch Dungeon Museum.

The Gaol plaque is in a busy spot in downtown Salem, across the street from a parking lot and garage that serve the mall, and kitty-cornered from St. Peter's Church. Even though the physical structure is gone, the emotional residues of those who were imprisoned in the Gaol, who visited their families there, and who worked there still linger in psychic space. If you can still yourself and shut out the noise of the modern-day city, you can tune in to the despair and anguish of those long-ago victims. The area quiets down a great deal at night, which may be the ideal time to travel into the past.

The Ropes Mansion

318 Essex Street

The stately Ropes Mansion (also once known as the Ornes–Ropes Mansion), with its beautiful gardens, has been important in Salem since its construction in 1727. It is near the Salem Inn and Witch House. It is said to be haunted by two of its famous Ropes family residents.

The house was built in Georgian style and was renovated in 1894 in the Colonial Revival style. It is listed in the National Register of Historic Places, and is now owned by the Peabody Essex Museum.

In 2009, the mansion caught fire and was closed to the public for repairs for more than a year. The grounds remained open. Even if the house itself cannot be visited, the gardens are worth seeing. The property sits on the "Judges' Line" (see page 49) and is considered to be one of the more haunted homes in Salem.

In its day, the mansion displayed the wealth of the three generations of Ropeses who lived there. The house was built for Samuel Barnard, a merchant. In 1768, Judge Nathaniel Ropes Jr. purchased the house from Barnard's nephew. The Ropes generations occupied the house until 1907, when it passed into a public trust.

The haunting activity dates to the lives of Judge Nathaniel Ropes Jr. and his wife, Abigail. In 1774, as colonial tensions were on the rise, Judge Ropes became unpopular for his Loyalist sentiments. One day, according to lore, a group of Patriots broke into the house with the intent of lynching him. He was suffering from smallpox and his health was so fragile that a decision was made to spare him. The lynching story may or may not be true, but Ropes did die of smallpox inside the house while it was being stoned by an angry mob.

Abigail met an unfortunate death in the house. One night in 1839, she passed too close to the fireplace in her upstairs room, and a spark lighted her long nightgown. Abigail burned to death, an agonizing way to die. (Long skirts and nightgowns catching on fire was not uncommon in earlier times.) Abigail's ghost, wearing a nightgown, wanders the upper floors of the mansion. Nathaniel's ghost also has been seen.

Tim McGuire of the Salem Night Tour relates that in the late 1970s, *National Geographic* was shooting photographs at the

Ropes Mansion for an article on its history and architecture. A photograph of a Victorian sofa revealed the mysterious ghostly image of the lower torso and feet of a man.

Salem Athenaeum Library

337 Essex Street

Libraries are often haunted, perhaps by ghosts who like to pass their otherworldly time in continuing education or entertainment. The Salem Athenaeum Library, which derives its name from Athena, the Greek goddess of wisdom, is located a short walk from the center of town, and not far from the haunted Ropes Mansion and Curwen House bed-and-breakfast. The library opened in 1810, drawing on a heritage established in the eighteenth century by two other libraries.

Nathaniel Hawthorne had ghostly encounters at the library. He frequented the Athenaeum every day to read and research, and became casually acquainted with a group of other regular visitors. Sometimes they would exchange greetings and conversation.

One of the regulars, identified by Hawthorne only as Reverend Harris, passed away. Shortly after his burial, Hawthorne was shocked to see the reverend sitting in his usual place at the library one afternoon, looking as real as he had in life. No one else seemed to notice him, so Hawthorne said nothing. For five consecutive days, Hawthorne saw the ghost, always in the reverend's favorite chair. The ghost was silent, and stared intensely at Hawthorne the entire time the author stayed at the library.

After five days, Reverend Harris vanished. Presumably, he decided to go on to the afterlife. His purpose in staring at Hawthorne remains a mystery.

I spent many hours at the library researching the witch and ghost history of Salem. Sometimes while in deep concentration on the second floor, I would feel as though someone were standing close behind me looking over my shoulder. I would turn around and, of course, no one would be there. Was it a ghost, curious about what I was doing? Or just a byproduct of my concentration?

Salem Common

Washington Square

The spacious and roughly triangular-shaped park near Salem harbor had at least one ghostly figure in it as early as the seventeenth century. Legend holds that the specter of Ann Pudeator, hanged as a witch on September 22, 1692, was seen wandering in the common area before her execution.

Like Rebecca Nurse, Pudeator was an old woman in her seventies at the time she was accused of witchcraft. Her second husband, Jacob Pudeator, had died in 1682, leaving Ann a good inheritance. Probably some of her jealous neighbors resented her wealth.

According to Mary Warren, Pudeator and several other defendants came to her and tried to persuade her to go to a feast with them. They said they had sweet bread and wine, but when Warren asked about the wine, they said it was really blood, and tasted much better than wine. Warren refused to eat and drink with them, and so they "dreadfully afflicted her at the time."

Sarah Churchwell testified that Pudeator brought her the Devil's book and forced her to sign it. Other accusations included: Pudeator stuck pins in the likenesses of three victims—Mercy Lewis, Ann Putnam, and Eliza Hubbard—and said they would be afflicted; she caused a man to fall out of a tree; she used witchcraft to kill a neighbor's wife and her second husband and his first wife; she turned herself into a bird. The testimonies were sufficient for the judges to condemn Pudeator to death.

Is it possible that her ghost was seen before she died? Such cases have been documented, though they are not common. The "ghost" is a person's double or doppelgänger (a German term meaning "double-goer"), an exact duplicate of the living person.

It can appear ghostly or seem to be solid flesh and blood. A widespread folk belief in England and Europe holds that seeing a person's double is a death omen.

The eight-acre common has been a public area in Salem since the town's beginnings. As early as 1685, it served as a shooting range used by men preparing for military service. Originally, part of the common was swampy with little hills and ponds. Farm animals were allowed to graze on the grounds. In the early nineteenth century, the ground was leveled off and drained.

Today Salem Common is bounded by Washington Square streets North, South, East, and West (one corner of the triangle is lopped, so that the park has four street sides). The Hawthorne Hotel is adjacent to one side. The common holds vendor and music festivals, and is a popular place for residents and visitors to relax.

People have reported seeing vague shapes move about the common in the distance at night, and have captured EVP and taken photographs with mysterious luminosities. Some stories hold that the ghosts of the old military shooters are sometimes are seen as well. The most active section is next to the Hawthorne Hotel.

If you visit the common at night, please be mindful of the residences that ring the park.

Salem State College Mainstage Theatre

352 Lafayette Street

Theaters seem to be especially haunted, and the large theater at Salem State College is no exception, at least according to lore. The story behind the haunting sounds more like urban legend, but nonetheless students, staff, and visitors have experienced ghostly phenomena associated with it.

The campus of the liberal arts college, more than 150 years old and the largest state college in Massachusetts, is not far from the historical heart of Salem. You can get there on foot, but it's a

long walk; taking the bus is the best transportation if you are without a car.

The 730-seat Mainstage Theatre is a public facility, and according to state law, must remain unlocked. The story goes that one
night in the 1970s, a group of intoxicated teenagers went into the
theater to fool around. They amused themselves by jumping on
the seats and cavorting about the stage. One, Tommy, went off by
himself into the upper level. The rest of the teens got tired of their
play and left, but Tommy had a fatal accident, falling headfirst
onto either the floor or the seats (accounts differ). He was killed
instantly. He was found the next morning by a professor.

Other versions of the story place the tragedy in the 1960s; the
kids are children, not teenagers, and no drinking is involved.
Tommy (also identified as Timmy) is twelve years old.

There is no historical documentation to validate the story.
However, there is a prankster ghost in the theater, believed to be
Tommy. He haunts the area above the auditorium, now used for
storage. He makes noises, moves tools and equipment around,
plays practical jokes, and causes minor problems in the theater.
For example, a student working the catwalk during a show was
constantly hit with small objects flying through the air, as though
someone was trying to distract her. The invisible presence also
pushed her spotlight off its mark.

I had the good fortune to meet a former SSC student who had
personal experiences with Tommy during the three years that she
worked in the theater. Ask any student, Bethany W. told me—just
about everyone on campus has a story about the theater's famous
ghost. Bethany was familiar with yet another version of the fatal
accident, and the identity of Tommy:

> When the theater was being built, it was open at night. It
> was right next to low-income housing projects. One night
> two little boys, about eight to ten years old, decided to play
> hide-and-seek in the construction area. One—Tommy—
> decided to go up into the catwalks, which were not finished.
> He ran along them in the dark, and plunged three stories to

his death. His young friend panicked and left him there, and construction workers found his body the following Monday.

All of these versions of the story feature the implausibility of a corpse lying unreported in a theater, but that's the nature of the stories behind many hauntings. Regardless of how or why a haunting takes hold in a place, it is a genuine phenomenon experienced by many people over a considerable period of time.

And for Bethany, the unexplained events were definitely real. "The first time I saw Tommy, I was a freshman, and I was running the spotlight for a kids' show," she told me. "That's when he was always the most active, during the shows. They did this one show all the time, and I think he was just sick of it. He would always make mischief. One night I looked over my shoulder and saw a little boy in a white t-shirt and jeans. I looked away and I looked back and he wasn't there."

Bethany thought she had seen a fast-moving, flesh-and-blood child. She asked other staffers, "Is there a little kid running around? I just saw a little boy in a white t-shirt and jeans. If you see him, get him out of the booth, because he shouldn't be up here."

But no one else had seen the boy. Later, Bethany learned that she had seen the ghost of Tommy.

"My second year, I did the same show. Tommy shut off the power just in the little room that I was in, which technically can't be done, because it is connected to the power in the other rooms in the area. But only the power in my room was off.

"The third year I worked in the theater—my last—I was running the spotlight and all of a sudden the pole that holds the light just dropped out from underneath it. I called someone to come into the room and turn it off for me. I put the pole down and then tried to raise it, and it wouldn't move. I called a professor, and the knob that holds the light was so tight that even he couldn't loosen it. There was no way it could have fallen being that tight, but it did."

Bethany told of a fellow student who was in the control booth programming the lighting for a show when she heard a little boy's voice call her name. No one was there. It rattled her so much that she left the theater.

Though the encounters can be unsettling, Tommy is harmless, Bethany said. "He just likes to play games. He's a kid."

Once he played games with a professor who was working in the theater alone at night. When it came time to leave, the professor went to a table where he had placed his key ring, containing the keys to his car, home, and office. The keys were gone. Thinking he had misplaced them or forgotten where he had laid them, the professor searched around the theater, the pockets of his coat, and even back at his unlocked office. Nothing. He was forced to spend the night sleeping in the theater. When he awakened in the morning, there were the keys on the floor smack in the middle of the stage.

Theater patrons sometimes hear ghostly giggling and the sounds of running footsteps in the hallway by the restrooms, which are located below the auditorium.

Tommy is sometimes helpful instead of pranksterish. Technicians who have worked on tall ladders say they can feel a pressure on their backs—perhaps it is Tommy lending them a hand to prevent them from falling.

Salem Witch Museum

19 Washington Square North

This imposing tourist attraction is located opposite the equally imposing statue of Salem's founder, Roger Conant—who, in his Puritan garb, is often mistaken for a witch by visitors. The museum, approximately thirty years old, occupies a former church. The attraction is a narrated show with mannequin displays of key scenes that recount the witch hysteria of 1692. The displays are lighted in sequence as the narration unfolds.

The museum has a large gift shop, and it is here that a ghostly presence acts out. Staff members privately acknowledge seeing books edge themselves off the shelves and launch into the air.

Sometimes the staff members who open up in the morning find books in disarray on the floor.

Salem Witch Trials Memorial
98 New Liberty Street

The Witch Trials Memorial is a small park next to the Old Burying Ground. It was dedicated in 1992 to the memory of the men and women who were executed on charges of witchcraft in 1692 (nineteen by hanging and one, Giles Corey, by crushing). The little park is bounded by low stone walls and decorated with twenty benches bearing the names of the victims, a quote from their last words or trial testimony, and the date and means of their execution. It was dedicated on August 5, 1992, by Elie Weisel, professor at Boston University and winner of the 1986 Nobel Peace Prize for his lifetime of humanitarian work.

The memorial is poignant, and visitors say they feel the spirits of the victims lingering through time and space as testimony to one of the gravest injustices in the history of America. According to lore, an unseen presence is always watching over the tributes left on the stone benches. Apparently this presence likes equality; if one victim receives a tribute, then all of them should. If a tribute such as a rose or stone is not left on every bench, mysterious lights appear in the memorial yard at night.

Next to the memorial park are two houses of note in relation to haunting lore. Neither is open to the public, but nonetheless ghostly activity has been reportedly seen in the windows. One is the Grimshawe House, at 53 Charter Street, once owned by the famous Peabody sisters. The gray-shingled house is vacant and in disrepair. Nathaniel Hawthorne attended a social event here in 1837 at which he met his future wife, Sophia. Hawthorne also featured the house in *Dr. Grimshawe's Secret*. People see lights in the windows at night when no one should be inside.

The Samuel Pickman House, located at the intersection of Charter and Liberty Streets, is Salem's oldest building, believed to

Salem Witch Trials Memorial

have been constructed in 1664. It is owned by the Peabody Essex Museum and used as administrative offices. The ghost of an unknown little girl has been reported looking out of the windows.

Witch Dungeon Museum
16 Lynde Street

The Witch Dungeon Museum is a popular tourist attraction that offers a live theater reenactment of events that took place during the witch hysteria of 1692, plus a self-guided tour through a recreated dungeon that housed the accused. The museum is located near the heart of the city. It occupies a building constructed in 1897 as a church. It was last used as a church by the Christian Science denomination. The museum has been in operation since the 1980s.

The theater reenactment is quite a treat, taking the audience back three centuries to experience some of the emotional drama and turmoil of a dangerous time. The dungeon features fifteen scenes recreating the old jail, Gallows Hill, Samuel Parris's house, and other places important to the 1692 witch hysteria.

Ghostly activity has been reported in the basement dungeon exhibit. A rocking chair in one of the scenes has reportedly rocked on its own. Visitors report hearing mysterious whispers and unexplained sounds. There is a legend of a spectral black "monk" figure seen in the narrow, twisting corridor, and his presence is especially felt at the replica of the fatal pressing of Giles Corey.

The Witch House
310 Essex Street

A trip to Salem is not complete without a tour of the Witch House, the oldest and only standing structure in the city with direct connections to the witch hysteria of 1692. It is also known as the Jonathan Corwin House, for it was the home of the witch trials judge by that name. None of the examinations of the accused took place there, but the house is reported to have ghostly activity.

Corwin was a prominent member of a wealthy family and heir to one of the largest Puritan fortunes. He made his money in the glory days of Salem's port, exporting timber and codfish to England and the East Indies. He owned merchant ships, wharves, and farmland.

Corwin bought the unfinished home in 1675 when he was twenty-four. He completed its construction, and he and his family lived there in comfort for more than forty years. The house was one of the grandest and most elegant in Salem, with three gables, a huge porch, enormous central chimney, and large, comfortable rooms. The house remained in the Corwin family until the mid-nineteenth century. Corwin himself is buried nearby in the Broad Street Cemetery.

After passing from Corwin family ownership, the house languished, and by 1944 was threatened with demolition when the adjacent street was to be widened. The potential destruction of this historic landmark helped launch a restoration effort throughout Salem. Citizens raised about $42,500 to have the house moved about thirty-five feet to its present location and restored to its seventeenth-century condition. It opened as a museum in 1948.

The house is a fine example of seventeenth-century architecture and furnishings; its architectural style is known as "First Period," the earliest style of New England. Even though no examinations or trials took place here, the exhibits do include information about Corwin's famous role in interrogating and condemning the accused.

Officially, ghost activity at the Witch House is downplayed, reflecting an attitude that paranormal enthusiasts find at historic sites and national parks. In December 2008, a nonprofit paranormal group from Rhode Island, Spirit Finders Paranormal Investigators, applied for permission to conduct a ghost investigation at the Witch House. Just a year before, the television show *Ghost Hunters* (also Rhode Island-based) had conducted an investigation at the Hawthorne Hotel, which had boosted the hotel's business. Supporters of the proposed Witch House investigation reasoned that such a hunt could also increase revenues for this historic property, already one of the most popular tourist destinations in town.

However, the city's Park and Recreation Commission denied the permit. One of the reasons cited was that if permission were granted to one paranormal group, then the city might be inundated with similar requests, given the popularity of ghost hunting. Opponents also said that approval might give too much emphasis to the paranormal, detracting from the historical significance of the property that Salem wished to promote. Paranormal supporters grumbled that the decision was hypocritical for a city that openly embraces its witch heritage.

Earlier in 2008, paranormal investigator Fiona Broome and psychic Gavin Cromwell investigated the Witch House for a television show, *Hollywood New England*. On the first floor, they sensed the presence of an angry man in a corner by a chair. Three other ghostly men arrived, apparently to discuss business with the angry man. They did not remove their hats, which Broome found odd, as this would have been quite rude according to seventeenth-century etiquette.

On the second floor, the investigators detected residual haunting energy of two females. One was a young woman who collapsed on the floor, apparently trying to hide a pregnancy. She may have been a servant. The second was a weaker imprint.

Staff members say they sometimes hear strange sounds when they are alone and closing down for the night. Footsteps sound upstairs, and sometimes phantom whispers drift through the air. There is sometimes the sense of a watching presence.

Witch Trials Site

70 Washington Street

The trials of the accused witches were held in Salem Town, now the city of Salem. The town had no formal courthouse, and no one knows exactly where the trials took place. The best estimate is near 70 Washington Street, and a plaque marks the spot, which is actually in the middle of the modern-day street. The seventeenth-century structures have long gone into a ghostly past.

Washington Street runs through the heart of town. During the day it is quite busy with traffic and pedestrians. The plaque reads:

> Nearly opposite this spot, in the middle of the street, stood a building devoted, from 1677 until 1718 to municipal and judicial uses. In it, in 1692, were tried and condemned for witchcraft most of the 19 persons who suffered death on the gallows. Giles Corey was here put to trial on the same charge, and refusing to plead, was taken away and pressed to death. In January 1693, 21 persons were tried here for witchcraft, of whom 18 were acquitted and three condemned, but later set free, together with about 150 accused persons, in a general delivery which occurred in May.

Try visiting the spot at night, and tune in to 1692. Visualize a somber room where dejected and dispirited victims faced stern judges. Their sole defense was their insistence on their innocence. Intense emotions such as anger, outrage, and despair become ghosts themselves. Can you feel the ghostly emotions of three centuries past?

Cemeteries

Broad Street Cemetery

Laws Hill

The Broad Street Cemetery is one of Salem's smaller resting places, but locals say it is the most haunted cemetery in town. The reason may be that it is the final resting place of one of the most notorious figures of the witch hysteria, High Sheriff George Corwin.

The cemetery was established in 1655 and is the second oldest in Salem. The cemetery sits on Laws Hill, a small mound, and is bordered by Broad, Summer, and Gedney Streets, a moderate walk from the center of downtown.

George Corwin—the son of Jonathan Corwin, one of the judges in the trials who is also buried at Broad Street Cemetery—exhibited great zeal and cruelty in pursuing the punishment of the accused witches, especially the pressing death of Giles Corey, who cursed him before dying. Corwin confiscated the properties of the accused, and reportedly kept much of the riches for himself instead of turning them over to the Crown. After the hysteria ended, Corwin came to be reviled and loathed for his role—so much so that when he died in 1696, his family buried him in the cellar of his home to prevent desecration of his remains. He eventually was reburied in the Broad Street Cemetery.

Floating lights have been reported bobbing through the tombstones at night, and some people even glimpse apparitions wandering about.

Howard Street Cemetery

Howard Street near 50 St. Peter's Street

The Howard Street Cemetery, once called the Howard Street Burying Ground, lies just across the fence from the Old Jail site. It is a jumble of old and crooked tombstones, many dating to the 1800s. The forlorn cemetery is said to be haunted, and its most famous ghost is Giles Corey, accused as a wizard in the 1692 witch hysteria and pressed to death with stones for not confessing.

In 1692 the cemetery was just an open field. There Corey was forced to lie down in a shallow, grave-like pit where he endured his final indignity of being slowly crushed to death. In 1813, a new jail (now called the Old Jail) was built adjacent to the area, and the cemetery and the jail stood side by side until 2010, when the jail facility was converted into luxury apartments.

Howard Street Cemetery

While the final resting place of Giles Corey is unknown, there is a long tradition that the ghost of Corey floats about the tombstones, touching visitors with an icy hand. Corey, who cursed Salem and its sheriff, acquired the reputation of a doom prophet as a ghost. Even Nathaniel Hawthorne was familiar with the legend that prior to any calamity striking Salem, Corey's ghost appears like a banshee foretelling disaster. "Tradition was long current that at stated periods, the ghost of Giles Corey, the wizard, appeared on the spot where he had suffered as the precursor of some calamity that was impending over the community, which the apparition came to announce," Hawthorne wrote. The ghost was reportedly seen before the Great Fire of June 25, 1914, that destroyed one-fourth of Salem.

Today the cemetery is dwarfed by the constructions of the modern era. It sits at a very busy intersection, and the constant traffic noise can interfere with attempts to get EVP. On one side stands the Old Jail facility, now renovated and expanded into luxury housing, and on the other side are homes. Across the busy intersection is a huge residential development. Daytime visits can be distracting. At night, one can observe the grounds even from outside the boundaries.

Old Burying Point

Charter Street

The Old Burying Point, also known as the Charter Street Cemetery, is the oldest cemetery in Salem. It is also the second-oldest known cemetery in the country. The cemetery is saturated in history and renowned for its spirits—in fact, some regard the cemetery as one of the most haunted sites in all of Salem.

The graveyard is located on Charter Street, overlooking the South River on a plot of ground that the town voted to set aside as a burial ground in 1637. There were probably already burials there even by that date, perhaps victims of the sicknesses that claimed numerous colonists in 1628–29. Little Charter Street, only two

Old Burying Point

blocks long, has so much history packed into it that it is listed in the National Register of Historic Places.

The Old Burying Point contains the remains of 347 persons, including famous individuals linked to the witchcraft trials: John Hathorne and Bartholomew Gedney, who were judges in the Salem witch trials; Nathaniel Mather, brother of Reverend Cotton Mather; and Mary Corey, the first wife of victim Giles Corey. Other notables interred here are Captain Richard More, who came over on the *Mayflower*; Governor Simon Bradstreet; Reverend John Higginson; and Chief Justice Benjamin Lynde.

Nathaniel Hawthorne liked to visit the Old Burying Point, walking alone deep in thought during the creative process of his novels. He would stop at different tombstones, and sometimes the names inspired him for his fictional characters. He used the name of his own ancestor, Judge Hathorne, of course, and also that of a Dr. Swinnerton, who appears with Hathorne in *The House of the Seven Gables*. Swinnerton also is in Hawthorne's unfinished novel *Dolliver Romance*.

Hawthorne put the cemetery itself in *Dr. Grimshawe's Secret*. Interestingly, the house at 53 Charter Street, now called the Grimshawe House, was the place where Hawthorne met his future wife, Sophia, in 1837.

People have collected EVP of otherworldly voices, and have captured mysterious phenomena in photographs, including ghostly shapes. Mystery lights and apparitions are also reported at night. There are unmarked graves in the cemetery, especially in the far right corner as you enter the grounds. Mary Corey's little tombstone, in the back center of the grounds, curiously faces in the opposite direction of the surrounding stones. Consult the bronze map at the entrance for the locations of specific graves.

On the other side of the cemetery wall is an eating establishment on Derby Street reported to be very haunted. The ownership and name of the establishment have changed a number of times over the years, lending strength to the lore. A curious story holds that a coffin and a piece of another coffin from the cemetery somehow became unearthed and crashed through the third floor of the establishment one night while a party was underway. There is no verification for this story, but it's a colorful bit of lore that adds to the atmosphere of the area.

According to lore, the eating establishment was once an inn during the early nineteenth century. A fire broke out. A woman and her daughter escaped and the husband remained to put out the blaze. They ran back in for him and were lost. Their ghosts reportedly haunt the cemetery and also the restaurant and pub next door. Mystery lights and apparitions have been seen in that part of the cemetery; there are unmarked graves there, too.

Today the Old Burying Point lies adjacent to the Witch Trials Memorial, a small park dedicated in 1992 to the memory of the men and women who were executed on charges of witchcraft in 1692.

St. Mary's Cemetery

Route 114

Saint Mary's Cemetery in Salem dates to the nineteenth century, and is widely reputed to be one of the most haunted cemeteries in all of New England. Numerous politicians have their final resting places here. The large cemetery is located on Route 114; one passes it on the way into Salem from Route 128.

Wander among the old headstones and soon the eerie vibe of the place settles into your bones. Phenomena reported by visitors include:

- Strange sounds, such as those made by an invisible dog running on the cement
- A sense of unease and foreboding on the grounds, as though visitors are unwanted
- Perceptions of being watched by unseen eyes
- Faint white lights that move about in the distance but seldom come close
- Feelings that one should leave in a hurry

Paranormal investigators have picked up EVP voices of men and women here.

St. Peter's Episcopal Church Cemetery

24 St. Peter Street

Apparitions have been seen in this cemetery, located in the center of town. The church was established in 1733 after religions other than Congregationalists were granted permission to worship in Massachusetts Bay Colony. The land was donated by Philip English, a man of French Huguenot descent who arrived in Salem Town in 1670 at age nineteen. English—his name by that time was Anglicized—married well to the daughter of William Hollingsworth, a shipping magnate, and became fabulously wealthy in his own right in shipping and trade. He was accused of witchcraft and jailed during the hysteria of 1692. Prior to that, he had been jailed for refusing to pay town taxes to support the Congregationalists. Philip was Episcopalian, which automatically set him apart from the Puritans; however, he and wife Mary did attend the Salem First Church.

English's wealth, foreign origins, legal disputes over land, and his disdain for the established church undoubtedly made him and Mary targets of the accusers. On the night of April 18, 1692, High Sheriff George Corwin and his deputies invaded Mary's bedroom and arrested her on charges of witchcraft. She agreed to go the next morning, and was taken to the Cart and Wheel tavern for interrogation. After three weeks in jail in Salem, she was sent to prison in Boston.

Philip was outraged and protested loudly. Warrants for his arrest were issued. He hid in a secret room of his home, and then fled to Boston to try to get Mary out of jail. He was not successful, and gave himself up. He was arrested and sent to join his wife in confinement.

The treatment in Boston was considerably nicer than that given to the victims in Salem, and the Englishes had only a nine-week wait for the trial. They were allowed great leniency because of their social and political status, and were able to leave the jail every day on their promise to return at night. One night they never went back, instead escaping to New York with the help of the governors of Massachusetts and New York. There they waited out the hysteria and the end of the trials.

They returned to Salem in 1693. Philip was enraged to find his estate plundered by the corrupt Sheriff Corwin, who had confiscated the riches of fourteen buildings, twenty-one sailing vessels, a wharf, and a warehouse. A year later, Mary died after giving birth to a son. English became an embittered man, and tried to recover his estate and damages from the Crown. He was given a paltry award.

English died and was buried in St. Peter's Cemetery. His donation of the land for an Anglican church was probably one of the few avenues of revenge open to him for the injustices done during the witch hysteria, as another denomination would weaken the stranglehold of the Congregationalists upon the population.

Legend holds that English exacted another, more personal, revenge by stealing the body of Corwin out of the basement of the sheriff's home. It is not known if that story is true—but it certainly would have been fitting under the circumstances.

The little cemetery at St. Peter's today has twenty-three grave markers. Philip's grave is one of only three known gravesites of accused witches in America. Some visitors have captured photos of what appear to be apparitions there. Perhaps English still haunts the land, looking for justice.

Danvers

Danvers State Hospital Site

1101 Kirkbride Drive

The site of the old Danvers State Hospital, also known as the Danvers Lunatic Asylum, is now private residential property. It is possible to drive up to the grounds and see the imposing, Gothic heart of the 77-acre development from the outside. The old facility has been reputed to be intensely haunted since the 1960s, and has ties to the witchcraft hysteria and to horror novelist H. P. Lovecraft. It is worth mentioning here because of its history.

The brick asylum was constructed on a hilltop between 1874 and 1878 at a cost of $1 million to $1.5 million, a staggering sum for that day. The site had once featured the house of Judge John Hathorne, built right at the top of the hill in 1646, and the home of the mother of one of the girl accusers.

When built, the asylum was viewed as a luxury facility, and local residents could not understand why such a beautiful place on such a stunning hilltop setting should be used for the insane, addicts, and others. Like many asylums, it was plagued with overcrowding and abuse issues over the years. It was originally built for 600 patients, but it housed about 2,400 at its peak of operation. Even though other buildings were constructed, the entire facility was strained. Patients included the criminally insane, drug and alcohol addicts, mentally handicapped, elderly, and others. Shock treatments and lobotomies took place. The facility closed in 1992 and remained abandoned for more than a decade.

The brooding building inspired Lovecraft to write about an "Arkham Sanitarium" in two stories, *The Thing on the Doorstep* and *The Silver Key*.

The asylum was reputed to be haunted by the ghosts of the patients from at least the 1960s. There are 768 graves identified where former patients were buried, their bodies unclaimed by relatives or friends, some of them noted only by numbers and not names (customary in the past at such facilities). Thanks to a citizen restoration effort, the remains in about half of the graves were identified and markers were erected.

In 2005 the state sold the property to AvalonBay Communities, which spent $80 million to convert the site into residential housing for people ranging from welfare recipients to the retired. Two-thirds of the existing structures were torn down. Part of the original Gothic building was turned into a recreation complex. The entire development has 433 apartments and 64 condominiums as of this writing. The development maintains the cemetery nearby.

In 2007, four apartment complexes and two construction trailers were destroyed in a mysterious fire, setting back the construction progress by several months. Some in town felt that the restless spirits of the dead were unhappy.

This is now private property, not the place to try to ghost hunt. The extent of any continuing haunting activity is not known.

Danvers Witch Trials Memorial

176 Hobart Street

The Danvers memorial to the victims of the 1692 witch hysteria was erected in 1992 on the site of the relocated Salem Village Meeting House, where civil and military matters were discussed and many of the witch examinations of the accused took place.

Not all of the accused were examined here, but the initial inter-rogations did take place at this site, complete with hysterical girls and horrified onlookers. The first group of the accused—Tituba, Sarah Good, and Sarah Osborne—was examined on March 1, 1692. There followed Bridget Bishop, Giles Corey, Mary Corey, Rebecca Nurse, and Mary Esty, among others. In 1702, the meetinghouse was torn down and moved to this site, where the lumber was allowed to rot into the soil.

The memorial includes Puritan symbols, the names of those who died, and statements made by eight of the victims prior to their executions. Witnesses report seeing strange lights and even full-bodied apparitions at the site.

Rebecca Nurse Homestead

149 Pine Street

If you have time to take in only one attraction in Danvers, make it the Rebecca Nurse Homestead. The grounds have three compelling reasons to visit: the original saltbox home occupied by Rebecca Nurse, one of the pivotal figures in the witch hysteria; a replica of the Salem Village Meeting House where examinations of some of the accused witches took place; and the Nurse family cemetery, where Rebecca's remains are buried—one of the few known burial sites of the executed victims. The homestead is located roughly five miles from the center of Salem.

Rebecca Nurse, born in Yarmouth, England, in 1621, was considered to be a pillar of Salem Village. She and her husband, Francis, leased a huge tract of farmland and did quite well for themselves. Francis was a tray maker, the builder of wooden objects for the household, a well-paying trade. The Nurses were regular churchgoers and models of piety. In 1672, Francis became constable of Salem Village, and he was often asked on an informal basis to help settle disputes. Over the course of his life, Francis was able to buy the farmland that he and Rebecca had leased.

Rebecca was seventy-one years old, not in good health, and bedridden much of the time when the witch hysteria erupted in 1692. Four women—Tituba, Sarah Good, Sarah Osborne, and Mary Corey—were already accused of witchcraft, and the accusations were rapidly spinning out of control. Ann Putnam Sr., the mother of one of the afflicted, cried out against Nurse. Putnam said both Nurse and Martha Corey were pressuring her to sign the Devil's book, and Nurse had beaten her daughter, Ann Jr.

It was a dangerous turning point in the hysteria. It was one thing to accuse a slave and the poor, but another to point the finger at one of the most respected women in the community. Nurse's reputation was spotless, and had cooler heads prevailed, the entire hysteria might have stopped right there. However, the Nurse family had tangled with the Putnam family in a bitter dispute over land, and Putnam boldly seized the opportunity to strike back.

Nurse was ill in bed when she received word of the accusations against her. In response to the news, she said, "I am innocent as the child unborn, but surely, what sin hath God found out in me unrepented of, that He should lay such an affliction on me in my old age." Forty citizens, outraged at the accusations, immediately signed a petition vouching for Nurse's purity—but she was still taken off to jail.

Another factor in Nurse's undoing occurred three years before the witch hysteria. Around 1689, pigs belonging to neighbors Sarah and Benjamin Holten got loose, ran into Nurse's garden, and tore it up. Understandably, Nurse was furious, and she marched to the Holten house and gave Sarah and Benjamin a frightful tongue-lashing. The Holtens carried a simmering grudge, and they, too, got their revenge when Nurse was accused of witchcraft. Sarah Holten testified against her neighbor, claiming that Nurse seemed to be unnaturally crazy while she was screaming about the pigs. Sarah also claimed that after Nurse departed on that day, Benjamin suffered a terrible stomachache. He deteriorated into fits of blindness, then took to "strange and violent" fits, and later died. It was damning testimony.

Mary Lacey Sr. testified that, at about the same time that Nurse was raging about the pigs, she had seen Nurse and five others baptized by the "Old Serpent" at Newbury Falls. The Devil, who carried Lacey there in his arms, "dipped their heads in the water and then said they were his and he had power over them . . . there were six baptized at that time who were some of the chief or higher powers, and that there might be near about a hundred in company at that time."

At first, it looked as though Nurse might be let go. Chief Justice William Stoughton went easier on her in her examinations than the other accused. However, every time he did so, Nurse's accusers and enemies went into fits and claimed she was tormenting them. In the face of unrelenting accusations, Nurse continually retreated to her faith in God: "I have got nobody to look to but God," she said in defeat, when she realized the tide was turning against her.

Nurse was tried on June 30, 1692. The jury found her not guilty, which set up a violent protest from both the afflicted girls and the courtroom spectators. Stoughton asked the jury to reconsider, and they returned with a guilty verdict. Nurse was condemned to death. On July 3, she was excommunicated, and on July 19 she was hanged. She maintained dignity to the end.

Fifteen years later, Nurse's excommunication was revoked, and in 1711, her family was compensated by the government for her wrongful death.

Nurse's sister, Mary Easty, was also among the victims, having been convicted and executed in September 1692. Another sister, Sarah Cloyce, was accused but not indicted.

Today the Nurse Homestead stands as testimony to one of the worst wrongs of the witch hysteria. It is owned and operated by the Danvers Alarm List Company. Set aside plenty of time for visiting, and plan ahead. During tourist season (June 15–Labor Day), the house is open Tuesday through Sunday in the afternoon, and in September and October it is open only on Saturday and Sunday afternoons. Openings can be arranged by appointment the rest of the year.

The house has had several additions since Rebecca and her family lived there. The interior can only be seen on tour. The tour includes an excellent fifteen-minute documentary about the witch hysteria, shown inside the recreated Village Meeting House on the property, which was constructed as a set for the PBS TV-movie *Three Sovereigns for Sarah*. Sitting inside the replica of the Meeting House brings home a real connection to the intense emotions of that turbulent time. After the tour, you are free to stroll the grounds.

The Nurse house has haunting activity. Staff members have experienced objects displaced from one spot to another without explanation. Revolutionary War reenactments are held on the property, and items in the house are moved to make room for reenactors who spend the nights inside. One time staff members moved a cradle upstairs; when they returned to the room a short time later, the cradle was back in its original spot. Apparently there is at least one ghost who doesn't like things to be rearranged. On another occasion, a rope latch on a door was seen swinging vigorously back and forth without having been touched, and without any breeze coming through the house.

According to one of the groundskeepers, female reenactors sleeping inside the house often awaken to the sense of an invisible presence standing over them. The groundskeepers live in an apartment adjoining the house, and sometimes they hear odd thumps and sounds and mysterious voices at night through the walls, coming from the empty side of the house.

Don't leave without taking the long walk down to the family cemetery, where the remains of Nurse and another executed victim, George Jacobs Sr., are buried. The exact burial spot of Nurse's remains is not known, for at the time the family would have kept the burial secret. It is believed that Nurse's family members retrieved her body from the mass grave at Gallows Hill in Salem Town, and ferried it by boat down the North River to the family homestead.

On July 30, 1885, the Nurse family placed an obelisk-shaped granite memorial in the cemetery and dedicated it to Rebecca's memory. The monument includes lines from the poem "Christian Martyr" by John Greenleaf Whittier:

> O Christian martyr
> Who for Truth could die
> When all about thee
> Owned the hideous lie!
> The world redeemed
> From Superstition's sway
> Is breathing freer
> For thy sake today.

In 1892, another monument was erected nearby, remembering and naming the forty neighbors who in 1692 signed a futile petition in support of Nurse's innocence.

Jacobs's grave is marked. His remains—or those believed to be his remains—were discovered in the 1950s during an excavation of the old Jacobs property in Danvers to make way for commercial development. The bones were put in storage until August 1992, when they were buried on the Nurse property by the Danvers Alarm List Company and the Salem Village Witchcraft Tercentennial Committee of Danvers, as part of the three hundredth anniversary observations in both Salem and Danvers.

In May 1993, a facsimile of a seventeenth-century slate gravestone was laid on the spot, bearing the words Jacobs is said to have stated during his examination: "Well! Burn me, or hang me, but I'll stand in the truth of Christ." The winged skull on his grave marker, a common motif of tombstones at the time, symbolizes the ascent of the soul to heaven after death.

If you have a recorder, try for EVP in the cemetery; some visitors have reported capturing mysterious voices here.

Sarah and Benjamin Holten's house still stands in Danvers at the intersection of Holten and Centre Streets. At the time of this writing, it was not open to the public.

Samuel Parris Home Site

Near 67 Centre Street

Nothing remains of the original home of Reverend Samuel Parris except the foundations. Visiting the "ground zero" of the witch hysteria, the place where it all began, is an eerie experience, however.

The remains are located near 67 Centre Street in Danvers. The site is set back from the street, accessed by a public cart path. There is no parking along Centre, so your best bet is to park on a side street such as Prince Street and walk to the path. The spot is easy to drive by; it is to the right of the private house marked 67.

The stone foundations mark the parsonage and an annex built after Parris was gone. The parsonage was tiny: a 20-by-42 foot, two-story, four-room house, with two living rooms downstairs and two bedrooms upstairs, and a half-cellar. The house was built in 1681. Ironically, the first pastor to occupy the house was George

Burroughs, who served as minister from 1681 to 1683. About a decade later, he became one of the victims of the witch hysteria.

After Burroughs, Deodat Lawson served from 1684 to 1688; he wrote the first book on the Salem witchcraft trials. Parris was the third minister of Salem Village, living there from 1689 to 1696. There followed Joseph Green, 1698–1715; Peter Clark, 1717–68; and Benjamin Wadsworth, 1772–1826.

Parris lived in the tiny house with his wife, daughter Betty, niece Abigail Williams, and slaves Tituba and John. In 1692, the year of the hysteria, a saltbox lean-to was attached to the house and used as a kitchen. The witch hysteria started here, with Betty and Abigail and their friends listening to the stories of Tituba and experimenting with divination.

As the hysteria got underway, the house became a focal point. Witches supposedly met outside the Parris home, according to testimony during the hysteria. Deliverance Hobbs, one of the accused, was interrogated in prison and confessed to being a witch. She said she attended a meeting of witches in the pasture near Parris's house. Among those present were Giles and Martha Corey, Rebecca Nurse, John and Elizabeth Proctor, Sarah Osborne, and Sarah Good. Reverend George Burroughs officiated, telling the gathering that they should slowly bewitch everyone in Salem Village, and they would succeed. He administered a sacrament of red bread and red wine that was like blood. The witches sat "seemingly at a table" to partake of it. Present was "a man in a long crowned white hat," presumably the Devil. Hobbs refused the food and wine and was threatened with torment. Goody Wilds urged her to sign the Devil's book in exchange for clothes and freedom from torment.

Hobbs's story, like most of the wild tales told by accusers and accused, was imaginary.

In 1734, Peter Clark added a separate, two-and-a-half-story study. By 1784, the parsonage was in disrepair. Wadsworth was given another piece of land, and he built a new parsonage there. He had the old one torn down. Most of the foundation stones were moved. The addition was also eventually sold and moved.

The foundation of the Samuel Parris home.

Nathaniel Hawthorne wrote that the workers had great difficulty in moving the addition, and were told by an old resident that the house was still under the influence of the Devil, and would remain so unless the roof was taken off. Finally the roof was removed and the house was moved. It remained at a site on Sylvan Street until the 1870s. The land at the original site reverted to pasture.

In 1970, Danvers town historian Richard B. Trask asked the property owners, Alfred and Edie Anne Hutchinson, for permission to do an archaeological dig there. Permission was granted, and the remains of the foundation were excavated. In 1988, the town of Danvers purchased the property and turned it into a historical site.

I spoke with a neighbor whose property borders the site, and he said he had never noticed anything strange. However, visitors feel the site is unusually quiet and spooky, and they collect EVP of mysterious voices. When visiting, please remember that residences are in close proximity, and respect their privacy and quiet.

Whipple Hill

Near 57 Forest Street

Whipple Hill is a spooky place opposite Endicott Park in Danvers. It is also known as Witch Hill. During the witch hysteria of 1692, the hill was supposed to be the nighttime gathering place of spectral witches.

The hill has hiking trails, and it is an easy walk to the top for some beautiful views. Visitors notice that the area has an odd and eerie feel to it; the atmosphere often feels "too quiet" and heavy. At night, strange lights are seen. The most haunted spot is believed to be the peak of the hill.

Lynn

Dungeon Rock

Lynn Woods Park

The ghost of a pirate mingles with the specters of Spiritualists and a pet wolf at Dungeon Rock, located in the 2,200-acre Lynn Woods Park. The story of Dungeon Rock is one of the more colorful local haunting tales, and is well worth a side trip from Salem.

The town of Lynn lies about five miles south of Salem. Plan a half day for an excursion and wear sturdy shoes for a moderate trail hike. The shortest path to Dungeon Rock begins from the Rose Garden entrance. Take a flashlight.

According to legend, the story of Dungeon Rock begins in 1658, when a black pirate ship sailed into the harbor of Lynn. Four pirates lowered a smaller boat containing a chest full of treasure. They rowed up the Saugus River, landing near the Saugus Iron Works. There they hid, leaving cryptic messages on the door of the Iron Works requesting shackles, shovels, hatchets, and tools in exchange for silver. The ironworkers complied.

The pirates settled in, making camp near the river; the spot is now known as Pirate's Glen. Their solitude was soon to be disrupted, however, when British soldiers discovered where they were hiding and raided the place. Three pirates were killed but a fourth, Thomas Veal, got away.

Veal managed to take the treasure with him. He found a natural cave deep within the woods and holed up in a new hiding place. No one disturbed him here; in fact, he became a member of the local community, and he repaired shoes for a living (why he did not use his stolen wealth is not explained in the legend). Veal even acquired a lady friend who would visit him in his cave with her pet wolf.

Veal might have lived out the rest of his life in peace, but disaster struck. An earthquake shook the area, causing the rocks around the cave to permanently seal off the entrance, burying Veal and his treasure inside. There would be no rescue.

Two centuries went by. The lure of buried treasure led to various attempts to break open the cave. In the 1830s, treasure-hunters damaged the cave mouth with powder kegs—but no riches were found. About two decades later, Spiritualism, mediumship, and contact with the dead were in vogue. In 1852, a Spiritualist from Charlton, Massachusetts, Hiram Marble, received a message from the long-dead Veal. The ghostly pirate promised him that if he would dig at Dungeon Rock, he would leave a wealthy man. Marble, a man of means, bought five acres around the ruined cave and organized a digging operation.

Marble made the quest for the treasure his central focus. Actually, he did not want the pirate's treasure for himself. He planned to use it to buy land for a public park. He also wanted to prove that communication with the dead was possible.

Marble moved his family to Dungeon Rock. He built a two-story wooden house for his wife and son, storage and tool sheds, and a never-completed building for visitors. Remains of those structures are still present.

Marble and son Edwin methodically pursued their digging and blasting of a tunnel. Progress was slow. They drilled holes in the rock, filled them with powder, and blasted away. The shattered rock and gravel was carried by basket to the hillside. The Marbles were able to clear about one foot per month.

The entrance to Dungeon Rock in Lynn Woods Park.

The work was expensive, and soon Marble ran out of his own money. The family started giving tours and selling bonds promising a share of the treasure. The place was popular with Spiritualists, who attended séances, held picnics, and went skinny-dipping in the Saugus River. The Marbles and the mediums consulted the spirits at séances for guidance in their digging. Hiram would write his questions on a piece of paper and wad it up; the medium would give the answers without looking at the questions. The Marbles religiously followed the advice, even when it meant changing the direction of the tunnel. The spirits kept reassuring them that they would be rewarded for their labors.

If there was a reward, the Marbles found it in the afterlife. Hiram died in 1868 and Edwin in 1880 without finding the treasure. The Marble family is buried near the rock.

Despite the lack of buried riches, Hiram's vision for a public park came true. After Edwin died, citizens of Lynn raised money to buy the land that is now Lynn Woods.

Today the entrance to the tunnel, tucked into imposing rocks, is sealed with an iron door. The door is unlocked during certain hours (check with park information), during which visitors can descend into the twisting tunnel. If you gain access, you will need a flashlight. Also, be aware that the tunnel floor is often wet and slippery.

Dungeon Rock is home to numerous ghosts: Veal, and, some say, other pirates; his lady friend and her pet wolf; and perhaps even the Marbles and their Spiritualist associates. Mysterious lights are seen here and in the surrounding woods at night.

Marblehead

Old Burial Hill

Orne Street

New England is chock full of spooky cemeteries, and the Old Burial Hill in Marblehead ranks near the top of the list. Marblehead itself has a spooky charm, and is well worth a side trip from Salem. The haunted cemetery sits atop a small but steep hill overlooking the harbor and the Atlantic—prime real estate enjoyed by the dead. A walk through the tombstones reveals why the land was unsuitable for housing—the ground is full of boulders. You can enjoy the fine view from a wooden gazebo or one of several benches.

Old Burial Hill was established on the site of Marblehead's first meetinghouse. An estimated six hundred Revolutionary soldiers are buried here, though only a handful still have their weathered markers. The cemetery has numerous interesting headstones, many still in good shape, carved with the winged death's heads that were customary of earlier times.

The graveyard also has a connection to Salem. It is the resting place—or restless place—of Wilmott Reed, the town witch who was among the last accused witches to be hanged in the 1692 witch hysteria. Reed and her fisherman husband lived in Marblehead, where Wilmott's witchy ways were well known and feared.

Perhaps she erred in publicly cursing people, not a wise thing to do in a superstitious society, and perhaps she might have mixed up some herbal remedies, which would have been common for the time. But a servant of Satan she was not. Reed was outraged at her death sentence, and her final words were a curse, "This town shall burn!" Salem did burn, in 1914.

After her execution, Reed's body was taken back to Marblehead and interred in the old cemetery. At night her angry ghost wanders the tombstones and streets nearby, shrieking her final curse, "This town shall burn!" A pond at the back side of the cemetery is named Redd's Pond after her (an alternate spelling of her name). Shadows are seen moving through the cemetery at night.

Other ghosts in Old Burial Hill are a one-legged Revolutionary War soldier seen stumping around at night, and a little girl said to have drowned in Redd's Pond in the 1940s. In the wintertime, people report phantom smells of wild roses.

There are three entrances to the Old Burial Cemetery. The main one is on Orne Street, a second is on Pond Street, and a third is by Redd's Pond.

Marblehead has numerous haunted places; local lore holds that the town is built on a "portal," or a place where the boundaries between dimensions are thin, and all manner of ghosts, spirits, and beings can pass through.

Another noisy ghost in the town is the "screeching lady" who haunts Lovis Cove and Screeching Lady Beach. The story is probably more legend than fact. According to lore, the screeching lady was an Englishwoman captured by Spanish pirates in the seventeenth century. She was wearing a valuable ring, and they could not get it off her finger, so they took her captive—an uncharacteristic, gentlemanly thing for pirates to do. Eventually they reached Marblehead, and decided to go ashore for some plundering. The Englishwoman seized the opportunity to escape and waded to shore. But the pirates found her and fell upon her, beating her savagely. They were finally able to take the ring. The locals heard her agonized screams but did not come to her aid. Her mangled corpse was found on the beach the next day. Supposedly, she was buried in the old cemetery.

Another version of the tale holds that a group of British pirates raided Marblehead. They found a wealthy woman on the beach; she was wearing an emerald ring that would not come off. They took her back to the ship, but more efforts to get the ring off were in vain. They then went back to the beach, where they cut off her finger and stabbed her to death.

The screeching lady is heard late at night and in the wee hours of the morning. Another version says that she screams on the anniversary of her death.

Bibliography

Boyer, Paul, and Stephen Nissenbaum. *Salem Possessed: The Social Origins of Witchcraft.* Cambridge, MA: Harvard University Press, 1974.

Burr, George Lincoln, ed. *Narratives of the Witchcraft Cases, 1648–1706.* New York: Charles Scribner's Sons, 1914.

Cahill, Robert Ellis. *New England's Witches and Wizards.* Peabody, MA: Chandler-Smith Publishing House, 1983.

———. *The Horrors of Salem's Witch Dungeon.* Peabody, MA: Chandler-Smith Publishing House, 1986.

Calef, Robert. *Another Brand Pluckt out of the Burning or More Wonders of the Invisible World.* Boston, 1697.

Citro, Joseph A. *Cursed in New England: Stories of Damned Yankees.* Guilford, CT: Globe Pequot Press, 2004.

Demos, John Putnam. *Entertaining Satan: Witchcraft and the Culture of Early New England.* 2nd ed. New York: Oxford University Press, 2004.

Forest, Christopher. *North Shore Spirits of Massachusetts.* Atglen, PA: Schiffer Publishing, 2009.

Guiley, Rosemary Ellen. *The Encyclopedia of Witches, Witchcraft & Wicca.* 3rd ed. New York: Facts On File, 2008.

———. *The Encyclopedia of Ghosts and Spirits.* 3rd ed. New York: Facts On File, 2007.

Mofford, Juliet H. *Cry "Witch": The Salem Witchcraft Trials–1692.* Carlisle, MA: Discovery Enterprises, 1995.

Upham, Charles. *History of Witchcraft and Salem Village.* Boston: Wiggin and Lunt, 1867.

Webber, C. H., and W. S. Nevins. *Old Naumkeag.* Salem, MA: A. A. Smith, 1877.

About the Author

Rosemary Ellen Guiley is a leading expert on the paranormal. She has researched and investigated a wide range of paranormal phenomena, including ghosts, hauntings, and spirit communications, since 1983. She has authored more than forty books, including nine encyclopedias, and hundreds of articles for a variety of publications. When she is not writing, Rosemary is on the road conducting investigations and research and presenting lectures and workshops. She makes numerous appearances in the media and on documentaries, docudramas, and radio programs. Her website is www.visionaryliving.com. Rosemary lives in Connecticut.